COME BACK *to* Yourself

LOVE LIFE, LIVE FREE

CHANEL F. DeGUZMAN, PhD

WEST PEAK PRESS • ANN ARBOR, MICHIGAN

Come Back To Yourself: Love Life, Live Free

Published by: West Peak Press, Ann Arbor, Michigan

Front Cover Design: AuthorSupport.com
Interior Design: LaTanya Orr, iselah.com
Editor: Rhonda Fleming
Author Photo: Davide Anderson, davidephotography.com

ISBN:978-0-9972949-0-3

For general information on our other products and services or to purchase books in bulk, please visit our website at www.chaneldeguzman.com

Author's Note: This publication is not intended as a substitute for the advice of health care professionals.

Printed and bound in the United States of America.

DEDICATION

For G.O.D.

Giavanni Olivia DeGuzman

Love Life, Continue to Live Free

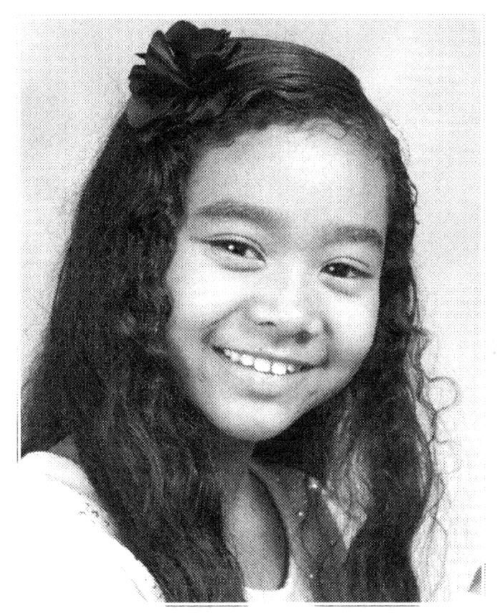

TABLE OF CONTENTS

FOREWORD

Hello, my name is Gian DeGuzman, and I would like to tell you about Dr. Chanel's book.

First of all I would like to tell you that Dr. Chanel has put her heart and soul into every word she has written. This book is your guide to being free, whole, and spiritually and emotionally healthy.

Dr. Chanel has spent months on this book and has included everything you need to be able to handle blockages in your life that push you back. The times I watched Dr. Chanel writing her book, she was very focused–that is unless my sister Giavanni whined for her to stay home–and she was also very diligent to write.

Writing was her main goal. WRITE WRITE WRITE!!!

While Dr. Chanel was writing her book, I was able to go with her one day to the "Shapiro" and she told me, "You can't interrupt me." With that she showed me that when she wants it done, she gets it done, because she has a real backbone (if you know what I mean).

As I sum this up, I would like to say that Dr. Chanel is an extraordinary person. Her hands have used her God-given gifts to write her book Come Back to Yourself: Love Life, Live Free.

I not only like to call her my Leader, but also my mother, Dr. Chanel Faith DeGuzman.

With love,
Her son,
Gian Mendoza DeGuzman

A WOMAN'S WORTH

by Chanel F. DeGuzman, PhD

Far more precious than fine diamonds and pearls
So beautiful and divine
Made from God's refined gold
A treasure to behold
A sparkle with brilliance unknown
A candle that beams the hottest fire
A scent that intoxicates
A soul that celebrates
A spirit waiting to unfold
Into the fullness of God for the world to behold
Her children long for her touch
Her husband's heart beats for her
The loveliest of all God's creation
Present with Him throughout eternity
Her worth measured only by the Truth within
Whose infinite value is yet untold
A woman's worth is hers alone
Guided and directed until Truth unfolds
Forever to be a daughter of the King.

INTRODUCTION

Do you remember what you wanted to be when you grew up?

As young children, we were driven by our imaginations. We would pretend to be a doctor or a mommy, an astronaut or a racecar driver, a fireman or a preacher. Sometimes all on the same afternoon. We role-played what we imagined our life could be like as an adult.

Children are amazing because they are free to believe they can be anything they want to be. And a lot of times what children consistently pretend to be ends up being their destined role in life.

But, unfortunately, a lot of us take the long way around to get there. And some never arrive.

What happens to us? Why do we stop trusting that voice inside us that told us as a child who we wanted to be? Who or what got in the way of us being our true self–of fulfilling our big dreams? What are we trying to prove and who are we trying to impress by pretending to be less than we are and someone we don't really want to be?

When I look at my seven-year-old daughter, Giavanni, I see a soul and spirit contained in a glorious body that is 100% FREE! She doesn't have to think about who is she. She just is. She knows what she wants and doesn't hesitate to ask for it–multiple times. And she knows what she doesn't want and is vocal about expressing it, however so politely, without being influenced by someone else's feelings.

She has her own sense of style and the only time her Mamma and Daddy try to alter it is when we have a "big affair" to attend. She's sweet and sassy but can spar quite aggressively with her 1st degree black belt brother. She is conscientious and smart and very caring. From the time she could talk, I had her daily affirm, "I am strong, healthy, and smart."

A friend of mine refers to Giavanni as "self-possessed." She owns herself completely. Currently she is not in an organized activity. When I questioned her last summer about what she wanted to do for the upcoming school year, without hesitation she replied, "I just want to be free."

I wish I could bottle up this self-possessed sauce of my seven-year-old daughter. I would give some to every woman who is holding back some part of her true self out of fear of what others will think. I would share it with every woman who is fulfilling another person's agenda at a fever pitch while not pursuing her own purpose. Every woman who is making her life decisions in order to appease others and make them feel comfortable.

I would give some to every woman who is shrinking back from her greatness because others around her feel threatened by it. To every woman bemoaning her weight or walking around wounded while still trying to have impact. To every woman who is self-medicating her secret pain with multiple glasses of alcohol, a sugar addition, too much chocolate, illicit or prescription drugs, or multiple romantic relationships leading to nowhere.

I want to share it with every woman tolerating loneliness and with every woman surviving life as an unhealthy workaholic.

But since there is no self-possession elixir you can take, I encourage you to read the pages of this book. Applying the concepts I share here will allow you to emerge healed, whole, and free, to be able to own your greatness and to live out your vision for your life at the highest level of yourself.

We'll start out (just you and me) getting you freed-up from the false version of yourself, so you can begin to create and attract from the true version of you. You will have a totally different perspective of your life and of your vision for your life when you're seeing it through the eyes of the real you.

You'll come to terms with your pain–your secret pain. Your wounds, hurts, disappointments, and your heartaches. If you never surrender to your pain, you can never be whole and free. It will take gut-wrenching inner work, but I'll be with you every step of the way.

You'll then do more inner work to forgive everyone and everything associated with your pain until you are no longer bound to anyone or anything. This difficult step is key to your freedom.

Now you'll spend time learning to "dance with your soul," fulfilling the longings you have buried, including those that you censor because other people might not agree. You now have the freedom to dance with your soul to your heart's content.

You'll redefine your mission and vision for yourself, leading to your self-actualization–"the achievement of your full potential through creativity, independence, spontaneity, and a grasp of the real world," as defined by dictionary.com. Your vision will be way beyond what others see, so you will need mentorship and support in order to own your greatness and live it out.

You'll spend some time making sure you stay healthy and well and taking time for yourself to rest, retreat, and renew. You'll also make plans to "steal away" and find time to "go within" for greater clarity and to stay committed to the deep inner work you've started–always going to higher heights and deeper depths.

I know many of you reading this book are looking for lasting, soul-stirring love. Well, once you do the work and come back to the real you, truer and deeper love is not far behind–whether you are single or are looking to deepen your marital love.

Lastly, you'll start to become conscious of the impact and legacy you want to leave and the explicit tasks you need to accomplish to make those around you successful. This is significant work but, like me, I'm betting there are people in your life and in the world you would love to see become whole and free.

We'll walk through all of this together, chapter by chapter.

I am a living testament of the radical difference doing this deep, freeing work can make in a woman's life. It was not easy, but I'm so glad I did it. I can't imagine missing out on what my life is like now.

I have come back to myself–the real me–and I'm living free. I love life and I am immensely in love with my husband, Gary. We have two beautiful, free children and a great family life. I make my health and fitness a priority. And I even beat my sugar and chocolate addiction.

And above all, I am fulfilling my vision for my life–I help women become completely free, live life at their highest level, and stop giving their power away.

It will take some hard work, but when you've come back to yourself, your life and your world will never be the same.

To be yourself in a world that is constantly trying to make you something else is the greatest accomplishment.

- Ralph Waldo Emerson

CHAPTER ONE

COMING BACK TO MYSELF

CHANEL'S STORY

I was the second child born in my family. Even at a young age I was known as "boss lady." I bossed my older and younger brothers and my younger sister. I did the majority of the cooking for them, and I did the disciplining - that is until my brothers became physically too big for me to do any damage. But don't get me wrong - our early days were fun and we enjoyed loving relationships.

Me? I was feisty. My grandmother, Ruth, used to call me Dirty Red. I was fun-loving, empowered, uninhibited and free.

That is, until one night when my world turned upside down.

I was nine years old and my mother was out of the house. Her boyfriend was babysitting and he decided to test the physical boundaries between him and me. At first I thought it was part of a game, but it quickly went downhill from there.

My perpetrator guided me along, using an unassuming approach. The sexual abuse went on for almost an entire school year. I finally summoned the courage to stop the abuse one day, on my own, as I was changing clothes for a tap dance lesson. As my perpetrator started making his advances, I remember continuing to pull up one leg of my tights at a time, ignoring his advances. He took my nonverbal cues to mean I was done with the abuse, even though I never verbalized a word. The abuse finally stopped in that moment. (Caution: I strongly advocate us empowering our girls and boys at an early age to scream, run, and tell someone if someone is making inappropriate advances toward them versus the nonverbal approach that I took.)

But even though the abuse stopped, the damage was already done. The major result was that I lost my way as a person. I was no longer feisty or fun-loving and I was certainly no longer free. I had lost my voice to say what I wanted or did not want from that point on. I think this was, in part, because my perpetrator never gave me a choice regarding the abuse (i.e., he took an assumptive approach). And even though he never threatened me into silence, I was still rendered voiceless as it related to the abuse.

I guess I was way too young to know how to handle this trauma, so I ran. I just started racing through life. I ran hard and fast– through classes, relationships, activities. I was always on the go. I did this racing unconsciously, in order to survive, never sitting long enough to let the pain of the abuse catch up with me.

Once I became a teenager, I became sexually active with boys. Predictably, I was repeatedly re-victimized in numerous relationships. My pattern became set: if a guy did not ask me if I wanted this or that, but just guided me along a natural course, I just succumbed and went along with it. That pattern went on for much of my college years and young adult life. I raced through my education obtaining four degrees: a bachelor's, two master's (simultaneously) and a PHD.

Fortunately, along the way, I landed my Mr. Right, Gary DeGuzman, although I was still racing. I started my career as a high achiever, never stopping long enough to let other people get to know me or for me to get to know them. I became utterly and completely exhausted; still I would rarely sit down.

Then, it all came crashing down.

Once I finished my doctorate degree, I decided it was time for the next thing: to start having babies. Well, we tried and tried and nothing happened. At our age, as my Ma Pauline would say, we were no spring chickens. So after about six months of no results, the medical advice was to start fertility therapy. We decided to start in-vitro treatments. As a result, I became pregnant with twins and we were thrilled.

On week seven, we went in for our doctor's appointment with not a care in the world. When the doctor conducted the ultra-sound, he discovered that one of the babies' hearts had stopped beating. Of course we were upset, but we concluded it would be okay. Perhaps handling one baby would be plenty for us. Well, certainly for me.

We came back on week eight only to discover the second baby's heartbeat had stopped. We were devastated.

I carried the lifeless babies inside of me for three weeks until our scheduled procedure to have them removed. I was awakened from the procedure by the tears pouring down my face. After I was brought to the recovery room, I asked to go to the restroom. I stayed in the restroom for what seemed like hours, crying and wailing, with my husband by my side. Finally, the nurses knocked on the door and helped me get back to bed.

The emotional pain I felt was unimaginable.

We made it home-I'm not sure how–and I cried for three days straight. I cried until there were no more tears in my tear ducts. It was the first time since my abuse that **I finally stopped running.**

I stopped everything. I didn't care about anyone or anything. I stayed with the pain for about three months: no work, no friends, no pretending, no nothing. I could not even connect with God in those early days after coming home. And I could not receive Gary's love.

Through several months of weekly counseling for grieving parents, I started to make my way back. I was finally able to reconnect with God and receive Gary's love.

While I did become more aware of making decisions based on what I wanted or did not want, I jumped right back in the fray, still on the run, and applied for a third Master's degree in order to get my teaching certificate. Fortunately, as soon as I received the acceptance notice, I learned that I was expecting "naturally," with very little effort on our part, I might add. Gary and I were thrilled and went on to have a beautiful, healthy baby boy.

I was still in individual counseling for ongoing support from the child sexual abuse. On what was my final counseling visit, I brought to the therapist's attention that we had not dealt with forgiveness. So she led me through a forgiveness exercise. Forty-five minutes later, my time was up. I was "cured." Not quite.

Feeling like I had not come to a full place of forgiveness with my counselor, I turned to my Pastor. He encouraged me to go to God with an open heart and a desire to forgive my perpetrator and let God do the true forgiving.

I immediately began to seek God with an open heart, ready to forgive. I just sat before the Lord. I don't know how long it took, but God gave me the ability to forgive. Every inch of unforgiveness that resided in my heart and body was wiped away. God's enormous presence completely saturated my heart and I knew I had truly forgiven my perpetrator.

What was even more miraculous was that God brought me to a place of cleansing my soul of unforgiveness toward everyone who had ever offended me–offenses that I never would have imagined needed to be forgiven. I was 100% completely free, completely whole in that moment. I couldn't believe it. Praise God. I was freed-up.

And, in my new freedom, I realized that I didn't have to race through life anymore. I could sit long enough to meditate and be in God's presence. The love in my heart today is even freer, even more expansive. I am so free, sometimes I feel like I could fly.

I went on to have a second baby. This fulfilled my secret heart's desire–to have a baby girl. Completely trusting God, Gary and I never found out the sex of either baby before they were delivered. She is truly a treasure and real, tangible proof, to me, of being completely free.

With this new freedom and awareness, I became bolder, more open to risks. I started going after what I wanted, being me, speaking in a powerful voice. I became more feisty, free to express the real me openly, fully and freely. This liberating feeling is like none other.

I am the feisty, fun-loving, free and uninhibited woman who was always there from the beginning. But I've had to go on quite a journey to come back to myself.

Now I live my life completely open, fulfilling my highest purpose–which is my assignment of opening a school and empowering young girls and women.

Now that you've read my story, it's time to find out where you are now, where you are headed, and then remove whatever is standing in your way.

Let's get started together.

There is no place so awake and alive as the edge of becoming.

- Sue Monk Kidd

SECTION 1

Let Go of What's Holding You Back

CHAPTER TWO

THE FALSE VERSION OF YOU

I'm not a perfect person, I make a lot of mistakes. But I really appreciate those people who stay with me after knowing how I really am. - Unknown

I am in awe of how beautiful women are.

We dress in our Sunday best from head to toe, style our hair perfectly, accentuate our best facial features with the latest makeup techniques, wear a gorgeous pair of shoes and carry a designer handbag. We look and walk like a model and project an image of dignity and refinement.

But some people have a more discerning eye than others. And those individuals are able to see past our façade. They can tell when what we're projecting on the outside is not who we really are on the inside.

When we begin to sense there's a chance we're going to be exposed, we just add another layer to our mask. This next layer is made up of attitude and assertiveness. And sometimes there's even some defensiveness thrown in.

> WHATEVER IT TAKES TO FIND THE REAL YOU, DON'T BE DAUNTED IF THE REST OF THE WORLD LOOKS ON IN SHOCK.
> *- Stephen Richards*

Another way we keep people from looking too closely is to pump up our résumé. We take on one more position, join one more organization, donate our time and money to one more charity.

This adds even more layers to our mask and keeps most people from questioning our motives–especially ourselves.

Who is this false version of you? How did you get this far away from the "real" you? Who are you trying to impress? And why?

What's wrong with being the "real" you? She is beautiful. And smart. Why can't you just be yourself?

So many of us have raced through life, never stopping long enough to ask the hard questions, much less taking time to respond to them. Questions like:

- Who am I?
- What is my purpose?
- What do I value?
- How do I want to live my life?

But we are responsive, aren't we? Some of us respond quickly to a man's sexual overtures. And some of us are responsive to a boss's request to use our skills and talents to further her agenda.

Yes, we get a little something in exchange, but we routinely undervalue ourselves because we don't recognize our true worth. So we give away an important part of ourselves in order to feel like we're being valued by someone else. This can happen in the boardroom or in the bedroom. In the classroom or on the playing field.

This false version of you builds a life from the outside, responding to the advances and opportunities created by someone else's vision and desires. While, on the other hand, the 'real' you would work from the inside out, declaring your own vision and desires that will, in time, create and attract opportunities that are a direct match to the 'real' you.

It all boils down to the fact that you are attracting people and opportunities at the same level as your current false version of yourself.

Let's look at a couple of different versions of 'false' women that are very prevalent today. See if any of the details sound familiar to you.

FALSE VERSION #1:

She got her degree and joined the 'right' professional and social organizations. She keeps her image polished and beyond dignified. She's a stand-out on her job and in her business community. She's beautiful and in reasonably good health. Her presence is noticeable from across the room. She's vocal and responds quickly and confidently.

But on the inside, she lacks the self-assuredness to go after the next promotion opportunity or to take a chance on living her big life dream. She has difficulty sharing her original ideas with her peer group. She carries a tremendous amount of stress around, which eventually ends up 'hanging out' in her body.

She works long hours a few nights a week–or at least she stays late at the office for appearances. She only sleeps 4-6 hours a night, often waking before the crack of dawn to tackle personal projects or work-related tasks. She answers emails at all times of the night. She can drink a little too much, but seldom has the opportunity. And she doesn't exercise consistently. If she's not already in a relationship, she suffers from loneliness, but won't open herself up to love.

FALSE VERSION #2:

She's pretty. She's smart. (Of course, I think all women are pretty and smart.) She grew up without a father figure in the home for most, if not all, of her life. She believes she needs a man to hold her all the time. But he can only hold her for so long without becoming aroused and wanting to have her sexually. She gives in—not necessarily because she wants to, but because she rationalizes that a man can't hold her without wanting and needing to have sex with her.

She may also rationalize the fact that she married someone she knows is beneath her, because she thought that if she didn't take him, then she was admitting someone lesser than her deserved him.

[Don't marry beneath you! And don't end up marrying a man just to avoid fornication. I'm not going to get into this, but don't have sex before you're married and don't get married to avoid fornication. You can wait.]

Some of these false women, version #2, ended up pregnant. Some of them got an abortion. Sometimes multiple abortions. Some of them didn't get an abortion and decided to have the baby. Then another. Then another. They work two jobs while their mother or grandmother takes care of their babies. And the main thing wrong with that scenario is that they think it's okay.

WHAT BOTH VERSIONS HAVE IN COMMON:

Each of these examples is looking outside of herself for fulfillment and meaning.

Version #1 spends her energy striving for success and ends up fulfilling someone else's agenda.

Version #2 looks for love and affection through a man or a baby.

Each one is overlooking the love that is already inside them. The strength, wisdom and power that each of them inherently possesses. They each give up their power to someone else and suppress their own life's agenda in exchange for either a salary or just to be held for 20 minutes.

> WITHOUT FREEDOM FROM THE PAST, THERE IS NO FREEDOM AT ALL.
> *- Krishnamurti*

I know this is harsh, but it's real.

One big problem is that today's society won't call a spade a spade. They just go along and pretend the false is the real. Therefore, we never deal with this false version of ourselves and get down to the real version. The real version of you is full of love, power, strength, faith and goodness. It's self-possessed and can have anything you set your mind to.

I know you may have been abused, hurt, discriminated against, raped, beaten, betrayed, abandoned, sodomized, kicked, overlooked, punched, ridiculed, attacked. You may have miscarried a baby, lost a child, lost a husband, lost a parent. All of you have experienced something hurtful. Living through any of these would be bad enough for you to remain wounded. But you don't have to. You were made to be whole. And you can be whole.

You can't move on and rewrite your story until you come to terms with your past–until you are able to shed the shame, guilt, and unforgiveness that keeps you just surviving–just barely keeping your head above water.

The exciting part is that you haven't given up. You're still surviving. You're strong. You may be tired and exhausted from the running, hiding, and shrinking, but you're still here.

Do you want to find the "true" you? Do you want to accomplish your life's work–work that will have impact? Do you want to fulfill the big dream you have for your life?

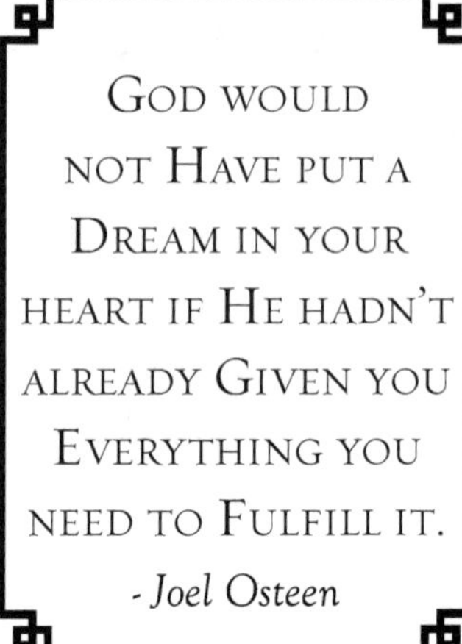

It is possible.

It's not too late.

You can do it.

But you have to start by acknowledging where you are right now. And you need to realize it will be a process to move from operating from a false version of you to the whole, thriving version of you–the real you.

It will take courage to lay down the façade, the one that's admired and respected by so many. It will take guts to stop the parading and pretending.

One of my coaching clients was talking about how hard it would be to let go of the false version of herself. She said, "It's all I have."

It may appear to you right now that it's all you have because you have invested so much in the false you. And right now, it's all you know. You've bought into the lie and you fear you would be a "no-body" without your mask.

But that's not true.

The real you is beautiful.

The real you is strong.

The real you is brave.

The real you has purpose.

The real you is smart.

The real you can be whole again.

The real you can be real again.

It usually takes a catastrophe for a woman to finally decide to come to terms with her façade and come back to herself. And this usually happens at the most inopportune time–like when I miscarried my twins.

But it doesn't have to be that way. You can decide today to start your journey back to the real you.

It will be a process. It will be difficult at times, because the false version of you will fight for control. But the real you is stronger.

Are you ready to come back to yourself? Then keep reading...

AFFIRMATION

I am beautiful just as I am.
I am more than enough just as I am.

TIPS AND STRATEGIES TO LET GO OF THE FALSE VERSION OF YOU:

- Observe those areas in your life where you know you are pretending and putting on an "academy award" performance. Don't judge, just observe.

- Observe those areas of your life where you have allowed yourself to be drafted to pursue someone else's agenda. Don't judge, just observe.

- Ask yourself, what are you getting out of it? If you don't like the answer, brainstorm ways you can make small changes in this area. Can you start to back off of your commitment? Do you need to recommit for another term?

- Start thinking about what's really important to you. Who is really important to you? Does your energy and time reflect this importance?

- Take a pause before you take on another assignment, volunteer opportunity, or come to someone's rescue. Say, "Let me get back to you." Really ask yourself if this is what you want. If you don't, say something like, "Thank you for the opportunity, but I will have to decline."

- Make a commitment to find or reconnect to the real you.

Once you go inside and
weed through the muck,
you will find the real beauty,
the truth about yourself.

-Lindsay Wagner

CHAPTER THREE

YOUR SECRET PAIN

Sometimes, the prettiest smiles hide the deepest secrets. The prettiest eyes have cried the most tears and the kindest hearts have felt the most pain. - Unknown

Some of the pain we carry around is visible, like a broken nose or the discoloration from a burn. But many of us carry around pain that is invisible, pain that can be masked and covered over. Marianne Williamson, an American spiritual teacher, author and lecturer, says that we don't know how to be any different.[1] Often the physical pain of the hurt subsides with time. For example, when a person falls, the pain from the initial fall is pronounced. But after rest and cold compresses, the pain continues to lessen.

Now, let's think about someone who is assaulted. Often after the bruises have faded, what remains is internal pain–pain that can go undetected and glossed over. Or when a woman has a miscarriage, which many women experience. Once her body has expelled the unborn fetus, the woman is left with emotional pain from the loss. This pain has to be dealt with.

In so many cases of miscarriage that I have personally heard about, the woman's resulting feelings are swept under the rug.

Often she returns to work after this "short-term illness" because she has recovered physically. But what about her emotional state? Many well-meaning family and friends try to encourage these women by saying things like, "It wasn't meant to be," or "You'll be able to have another one," or "A lot of women have gone through it." Women internalize these common sentiments and discount how they really feel.

When I miscarried twins, I didn't allow anyone, including my husband, to comfort away my pain. When people called on the phone, I didn't cheer up. I didn't try to sound like anyone other than who I was in that exact moment. I didn't go back to work for nearly eight weeks. My husband and I started grief counseling and slowly I made my way back. This incident was the very first time in my life that I stopped pretending and quit putting on a face to look as if everything was fine–because clearly it wasn't.

I was not going to let anyone rob me of the pain that I needed to experience for as long as I needed to experience it. I needed to feel that pain. Some will say, "Well, I can't take that much time off to recover from an illness that employers don't seem to think is that traumatic. Because physically, I probably could return to work within a couple of weeks if not sooner." This is where it's important to own your pain and not turn it over to others and allow them to decide how you're feeling or not feeling. It's your damn pain anyway! Honor yourself and feel your pain so that you can recover from it.

For many of us our pain is buried in our comfortable lifestyle or what I like to term the "great cover-up." It masks a dull pain that we have internalized and accepted as normal. We drive nice cars, wear stylish clothes, go on vacations, go to the theater, and work at relatively good jobs with good incomes. However, our soul longs for a deeper, richer life experience, one where we know our true purpose and we are actively pursuing it. Life lived at a level where we feel passion and love from our soul's core.

> When your Soul is singing in Joy, then you Know you are Doing it Right.
> - *Abira Mukherjee*

Here's what so many of us do. We medicate the pain until we can't feel it anymore. How do we do this? By drinking alcohol, smoking marijuana, taking drugs, having sex, watching mindless TV, starting a new relationship, taking on a new job, and immersing ourselves in our work. You name it, we'll do it. We'll do anything possible to avoid the pain. Guess what? The more you suppress the pain, the more your tolerance for the pain grows, and the more and more medication you will need to get the same relief. Can you see that it's a downward spiral?

What's left of your wound is a scar with a scab that gets harder and harder, coarser and coarser, until it fuses into and becomes a part of who you are. Anytime you think of the pain or you experience a trigger, you reinforce the scarring.

Have you ever tried to do a fully extended stretch when you have a scar? Probably not, because you are very conscious of your scar and you'll do almost anything to avoid someone bumping into it or having the scar tear open. So you become guarded, careful, not fully extending that part of your body to keep that scar from tearing, bleeding, and your having to go through the same process all over again. "No way, no how am I going through that again!" So you pull back, withdraw, lessen, become small, avoid, cover, and protect.

Tell me how you can create, produce, excel, and thrive when you've numbed yourself just so you can survive? Just so you can go to work and take care of the kids. Just so you can make it through another day, another month, another year. Let's face it, you can't! But you can expend a lot of energy trying to make it look good.

What if you took that same energy and devoted it to identifying the pain–the true source of the pain–uncovering and exposing it–no matter how old it is or how painful it may be?

Some of us try to plunge ahead and do deep, meaningful, worthwhile work, but not from a place of our whole selves. When we do this, we just stretch the scar. We take the pain and the scar with us into our "holy" work. And we are shortchanging ourselves and those we serve by trying to do this worthwhile work "half-baked."

Change is going to hurt. Let's get that out of the way now. You may cry, scream, want to fight, hurt. All of these are normal feelings that we use to suppress, to stay in control. But I guarantee you, you'll have to face your pain one day, either under force or voluntarily. So my strongest recommendation is to deal with your pain on your own terms, not when an unexpected event happens and you don't have a choice in the matter.

We are always presented with situations that lead us to our higher good. We, however, have the free will to decide if we will take advantage of the opportunity that has been presented to us. We are always in control and can make changes either under immediate duress or when we make the conscious decision that we're ready to make the needed change on our own terms.

Over time, when you stuff the pain into your body and into your cells, your body accepts the stress as normal and dis-ease often results from the overtaxation of the great cover-up. Think about how many of us eat to suppress the pain. Our body goes into overdrive when we overeat or eat an unhealthy, unbalanced diet.

Think about drug users. Not only does the drug affect their body and organs negatively, but it actually creates dependency on the drug and the habit of turning to something external to ease their pain. Again, it will take more and stronger doses to get the same fix, high, relief.

There is a way to lessen the dependency on the external. It's by going within. Identifying the pain and learning a process to finally surrender the pain, forgive anyone and everything attached to the pain, and move to full liberation. This is where you can create, thrive, inspire and move into deep spaces without the potential to re-tear the original scar.

Think about the difference you will experience in your life once you finally surrender the pain and build a new life in place of the scarred, wounded you.

Life is full and it's waiting for the full expression of you and all that you have to offer to it. Those individuals who need your genuine touch, emotion, and love are waiting, too. Are you ready to open up and be free? Let's keep reading.

Here are the concrete steps you need to take to surrender the pain, detach from the associated emotions, and move to forgiveness to finally be free.

> WHAT IS TRUE IN BUSINESS, CHURCHES AND INDIVIDUAL RELATIONSHIPS IS THAT WE ARE ONLY AS SICK AS OUR SECRETS.
>
> - *Rev. Guy Lynch*

Step 1: Identify the wound

Each of us has experienced some type of pain, hurt, disappointment, betrayal, defamation, physical abuse, mental, emotional, and verbal abuse, abandonment, death of a loved one, mistreatment, senseless violence, and the list could go on. However, there is nothing new under the sun. While each experience is personally unique to a particular individual, nothing should come as a surprise. We are not going to judge the severity of one pain over another.

As I mentioned earlier, never allow anyone to judge or invalidate your pain. It all hurts and many of us have gone to great lengths to avoid feeling the pain for various reasons. However, in order to be free, we have to come to terms with the pain we harbor. For many of us it is "secret pain," the kind of pain we don't want anyone to know about. For example, I rarely told anyone that I experienced child sexual abuse and I outran my pain because I never wanted to be associated with "that" kind of experience. It will take some serious introspection on your part to name the pain and the source behind the pain–which could be you.

Please spend some time now identifying your emotional scars and hurts. Write them down.

Step 2: Understand how you became so intertwined with the hurt and wound

In his book, ***The Confidence Gap***, Russ Harris tells us that in order to "unhook" and detach from the emotions, hurts, and wounds of your past, you need to clearly understand how you became intertwined with them in the first place.[2]

Joe Dispenza says that the end product of any experience is an emotion.[3] Think about the emotions that are tied to the people and places and things you have experienced, both the good ones and the bad ones.

Often times we have bonded energetically with another person so much that our energies are interwoven. When one person feels anxiety, inferiority, or depression, we become connected with that same energy, perhaps not at the same frequency as the originating person, but we have indeed fused and bonded. Often we bond with certain people through survival-oriented emotions (e.g., competition, lust, guilt, shame, fear, doubt, anger, hate, judgment, etc.), making it that much harder to break free from negative experiences.[4]

During a rough restructuring period in a company where I was employed, I had come to depend on the warm-hearted, positive energy of another staff member. Every time this person would take days off, I would always welcome him back and feel a sense of relief, because he was a constant, a rock.

Well, one day out of the blue (at least for me), he emailed the team to inform us that his last day would be in three weeks. As I read the email, I let out a loud squall of panic. I couldn't believe it. What would I do without this person's good nature? At first I could not understand why I was having such a tangible reaction. I even became teary-eyed. Well, I had energetically bonded with this person for survival during the restructuring of our team a couple years earlier, and for sustaining energy after the restructuring, during the settling-in process.

At the first discovery of my colleague's news, I could not work the rest of the day and went home within a couple of hours and even took an additional day off to "recover" and regroup. When we become attached to people through survival, is it any wonder why it's difficult to leave an unhealthy relationship? Let alone a positive one? Be very mindful and conscious of the individuals you allow yourself to connect with energetically.

Now that you have identified the wound and how you became bonded to it, for good or bad reasons, it is now time to understand the costs of carrying around the hurt and wounds.

Step 3: Understand the costs of carrying around the hurt and wounds

The very emotions and feelings that are a result of the past hurts and wounds are being filtered and transmitted through each and every cell before it is released; therefore, if you are holding resentment, unforgiveness, anger, and hurt, you are the one being harmed. Because those emotions are trapped energy in your body, you are actually a filtering machine. The past experiences generate emotions that are internalized, regurgitated, and spewed back, as you release them, out through your cells and body.

As we discussed in Chapter 2, *The False Version of You*, you are currently attracting love, relationships, health, wealth, and a lifestyle at your current level of consciousness, which contains weight, baggage, and trapped energy from past hurts and wounds. You are attracting at the "false-version" of you, not your freed-up, best self. Therefore, you are likely to keep falling into similar situations that recreate or allow you to reenact at the current level of your consciousness.

The cost of not being freed-up is you are spinning your wheels, recreating experiences that are not serving your heart's desire or your highest good. Physically, you can be weighed down so much that your energy is de-elevated by survival emotions that vibrate more slowly and are denser.

"Emotions are energy in motion." When you hold on to survival emotions, your body becomes full of density and mass and there is less space for vital energy.[5] Can you see why you may not have the energy to participate fully in life, to be healthy, and to pursue your purpose with vigor?

It is now time to detach energetically and emotionally from the lower density emotions that have you in bondage. How do you do that? Keep reading.

Step 4: Detach from past emotions

Get in touch with the source of the pain, the emotion of the pain, wound, or scar. Don't resist "going there." We are exposing the root cause so you can detach from it.

Your thoughts lead you to feel a certain way. Think about the thoughts you have that have been associated with the pain. In my case of overcoming child sexual abuse, I didn't have any thoughts because I was too busy running away from the pain, until I became conscious that I was, in fact, running and racing. Then, I began to just notice when I was engaged in this behavior. I did not judge what I was doing; I only observed and noticed.

Once you start the process of observing and noticing and becoming aware, you can start to detach and "unhook" from the emotion that is causing the pain. When there is physical pain involved with the abuse, it is often after the physical pain subsides that the emotional pain that remains gets buried.

One way to detach from the emotion is to mentally put a thought that surfaces in this detachment process on a leaf and watch that leaf float down a calm widening river that eventually goes over a waterfall, never to be seen again. Then when the next thought comes, put that thought on a new leaf and watch that leaf float down the river. Repeat as often as the thoughts surface.

Also know that we can't stop thoughts from entering our mind, and there are triggers that remind us of situations and experiences that will bring the thought to the top of our minds. Simply acknowledge the thought--oh, it's you again, hello–and send it on its way, calmly and unengaged.

During childbirth preparation, I was actually taught that for each "sensation" (i.e., labor pain) that would come, I should feel it fully, give in to it, and know that I would never see that "sensation" again. I kept taking each labor pain the same way: embracing it fully, letting it go, and knowing that I would never see the pain again. After repeatedly doing this, a baby emerged and there were no more labor sensations.

Another way to detach from your thoughts that surface is to take your thoughts with an associated pain and let the thought sink to the bottom of the ocean, calmly and effortlessly, detached and unencumbered. Just watch it descend and leave it there.

The more you practice the process of detachment, the less and less you will have the thoughts and associated emotions and pain. They will take up residence where you send them but there will no longer be a cozy home for them in your body, mind, heart or soul.

Here's another way to disassociate and disengage from your thoughts and pains: reassign them another meaning or write a different story about the experience. Here is an example. When my title was eliminated and my job duties were drastically decreased, I withdrew in a very visible way. For a time, I only contributed what was needed, which still ended up being above average. However, I knew I was affected.

In order to get to a new place in my growth, I had to detach from "what I perceived was done to me" and to depersonalize the experience. My new story or rationalization was that the move was a business decision, nothing more and nothing less. In fact, in the big picture, it was the impetus I needed to commit to my craft of empowering and inspiring women to be free, to keep my emotions and energy available for my projects. It was also the impetus to not be intertwined with the energy of an organization who was "sold out" to its mission, as its members should be. I remained in my position not because I was "sold out" to its mission but for a paycheck.

Here is the valuable lesson I learned: Don't get intertwined with people, companies, and situations for a paycheck. Don't compromise your talents and gifts. Instead, be intertwined with the work that lights a fire in your soul, fuse energetically with a person who is available to you and who has the capacity to connect with you at the level you desire.

Step 5: Forgive everyone, everything, now and forever who was/is associated with the pain

Deep down, I think most of us know we have some forgiving to do in order to be whole and free. In all my years of counseling to "manage" the effects of the child sexual abuse, none of my therapists ever brought up the need to forgive.

However, instinctively I had an inner sense that forgiveness was necessary in order for me to be freed-up and whole. And I love the way The Free Dictionary defines "whole": *Containing all components; complete. Not divided or disjoined. Not wounded, injured or impaired. Sound or unhurt.* That's how we want to live.

The process of forgiveness or becoming freed-up is so important that I would like for you take a break and reflect on the five steps you just read before we take a deep dive into the next chapter devoted exclusively to forgiveness.

AFFIRMATION

I freely surrender my secret pain and
I am ready to be whole and free.

TIPS AND STRATEGIES TO SURRENDER YOUR SECRET PAIN:

- Make a private list and write down any offense, small or large, that you recall. Then write down the person(s) or group(s) involved in the offense and the emotions attached to the offense. Hold this list until we do our work in the next chapter on unforgiveness.

- Make a commitment to relinquish and surrender your secret pain.

- Become conscious and notice the ways you keep your pain "at bay" or how you self-medicate your pain so you don't have to feel it. Don't judge how you deal with your pain.

- Go through the five steps to relinquish and surrender the pain:

    1. Identify the pain, hurt, wound, sorrow.

    2. Examine the ways you have become intertwined with the emotions from the pain.

    3. Count the cost to your health, well-being, and future purpose that you experience by holding on to the pain.

4. Use the detachment techniques to "unhook" from the emotions associated with the pain. (Place thoughts and triggers associated with the pain on a leaf and watch it float down over a waterfall and reassign the associated pain another meaning.)

5. Forgive everything and everyone, including yourself, now and forever, of both intentional and unintentional offenses associated with the pain. (See next chapter on the forgiveness process for help with this one.)

We must embrace pain and burn it as fuel for our journey.

-Kenji Miyazawa

CHAPTER FOUR

UNFORGIVENESS

You will begin to heal when you let go of past hurts, forgive those who have wronged you and learn to forgive yourself for your mistakes. - Unknown

Your soul cries out to be free, to breathe fully, to love and to feel deeply. Forgiveness is key to your complete healing and the freeing of your soul.

You have spent a good amount of time in the previous chapter letting go of your secret pain. Now we have come to the point where we will go through the forgiveness process together, in love and with full support, completely expecting to reach a place of peace and inner calm that comes as a result of forgiveness.

It is important to note that forgiveness is a process, so please be patient with yourself. Stay with it until you can boldly say that you have forgiven everyone and everything, both now and forever, of both intentional and unintentional offenses, and you are completely whole and free (Teachings of the Rev. Ron D. Coleman. Sr., Founder and Former Senior Minister and Pastor of God Land Unity Church).

You are not alone in your desire to experience forgiveness. Sixty-two percent of Americans agree (strongly or somewhat) that they need more forgiveness in their personal lives.[1]

FOR THE LORD IS THE SPIRIT, AND WHEREVER THE SPIRIT OF THE LORD IS, THERE IS FREEDOM.

- 2 Corinthians 3:17 NLT

We're going to start with an overview and definitions of forgiveness and unforgiveness. But before we look at how forgiveness works, please take a minute and go back to the previous chapter, **Your Secret Pain**, and review the concrete steps you need to take to surrender the pain and detach from the associated emotions.

OVERVIEW OF HOW FORGIVENESS WORKS

Once you identify the emotion that was attached to the hurt, wounds, and scars of your past and detach from it, we need to apply God's pure love to the wound. What is pure love? God.

. . . God is love. 1 John 4:8 (ASV)

How do you apply God's love to your wound? You must seek God and His Presence, His Spirit. God will wash you all over with His purest love, but you must avail yourself of His Presence.

For the Lord is the Spirit, and wherever the Spirit of the Lord is, there is freedom. - 2 Corinthians 3:17, NLT

In God's presence there is pure love, the kind of love that will saturate your heart and every cell of your being until there can be no unforgiveness that prevails. It takes practicing the Presence of God (seeking the Spirit of God) daily to embody God's love. Seeking the Presence of God means to set your mind and heart to continuously be conscious of the Lord your God (1 Chronicles 22:19), to quiet down all of the externals and go within yourself, where God's Spirit resides. Once you embody God's love, it permeates your very existence.

When you embody something, you take it in as your own; you mirror, envelop, personalize, epitomize, express, and incorporate it into your being. At that point, there is nothing generated on the outside of you that can hold you hostage, tie up your emotions or have you operate from a reactionary, survival instinct. As you are freed-up, you are able to forgive everyone for anything, forever.

To epitomize the love of God, you must take God's love in every day. You become a living, breathing energy of pure love. This is how you are able to stay freed-up.

Forgiveness is the healing you obtain through the love of God. It is God's unfailing love working through you that allows your heart to forgive. As you continually renew your mind daily and renew your alignment to God's presence and His love, you will not reattach yourself to the emotional hurt or wound. Since there is no more energy given to the hurt, it gradually subsides.

Here's how I like to think about it. Your painful wounds are like strong ocean currents crashing toward the shoreline. But the more of the ocean (God's healing love) they have to travel through, the more their energy dissipates, until they finally die out as a calm wave gently washing up on the shore. Your only role is to decide to detach, decide to become free, and let the healing of God's love penetrate your wound until the pain is eradicated.

The hurt is just an instrument; it's neutral. I know that's not easy to hear, but I'm trying to get you to come up higher, to a level where you've never been before because you won't take off the training wheels.

You continue to fuel the hurt with emotion that gets replayed over and over until over the years you have built it a nice comfy home. Trust me; it will fight you tooth and nail not to give up that cushy home you have built. But if you want to be free, you have to evict it! Serve the notice and get started with the eviction process.

> EMBODY THE FRUIT OF THE SPIRIT WHICH ARE LOVE, JOY, PEACE, PATIENCE KINDNESS, GOODNESS, FAITHFULNESS, GENTLENESS, SELF-CONTROL.
>
> *- Galatians 5:22-23 ESV*

Do you have an older person in your family who is bitter? Every time you are around them, they bring up the past and all the people who have offended them or owe them money. Can you see how those emotions are trapped in their body's cells, and how it can lead to dis-ease? This person is not freed-up because the emotions (e.g., anger, resentment, bitterness, etc.) serve to remind them of who they are. And without that awareness, they fear they would become a "no-body".

Instead, we want to "em-body" new emotions (e.g., love, joy, peace, goodness, forgiveness, faithfulness) which are designed to bring us closer to God, our Creator.

When you are aligned with God, you become a co-creator. You are no longer living to reenact the past, but you are now free to create a brand new future. Behold, you become a new creation.

God's love is the ointment you must generously apply until there is no more negative emotion attached to your pain and stored in your heart and cells. Are you willing to relinquish the past, the hurt, and the unforgiveness? Are you willing to forgive everyone, including yourself, for everything and anything, from the past right up to this present moment?

You cannot hold unforgiveness and love simultaneously. Know that where you are still holding negative emotions is the extent of your compassion. If there is someone you simply can't forgive, it is a sure sign of where your compassion ends.

The lesson of unforgiveness is not about the hurt or the other person. It is about whether you will trust that God can and will eradicate all unforgiveness, if you will open up your heart and let Him do the work.

DEFINITIONS

Forgiveness

1. "Forgiveness is giving up the hope that the past could have been any different." - Oprah Winfrey

2. "Forgiveness is a response to the experience of being hurt or offended within an interpersonal relationship."[2]

3. OxfordDictionary.com says "forgiveness" means "to stop feeling angry or resentful toward (someone) for an offense, flaw, or mistake."

So unforgiveness means holding anger, resentment, bitterness, and hatred toward another person, yourself, or a circumstance.

The Costs of Unforgiveness

The most egregious effect of unforgiveness is the damage it causes to your inner spirit and soul. Unforgiveness is like a cancer because it eats away at its hosts, namely you.

Dr. Steven Standiford, chief of surgery at the Cancer Treatment Centers of America, found that "Harboring these negative emotions, this anger and hatred, creates a state of chronic anxiety," he said. "Chronic anxiety very predictably produces excess adrenaline and cortisol, which deplete the production of natural killer cells, which is your body's foot soldier in the fight against cancer," he explained.[3]

Karen Swartz, M.D, similarly noted that when individuals harbor chronic anger (unforgiveness) it leads to changes in blood pressure, depression, increases anxiety, and affects the immune system. A weakened immune system reduces the body's ability to fight off diseases, including cancer. Conversely, forgiveness is associated with multiple health benefits including decreased blood pressure, improved cholesterol, stress and anxiety levels, and lowering the risk of hearts attacks.[4]

Unforgiveness negatively affects relationships with loved ones most of all. My pastor cautioned me at the hospital when my younger sister passed away to be aware of all sorts of issues that can surface during this time. I was a little surprised by his warning, but it proved to be true.

> DON'T ALLOW YOUR WOUNDS TO TRANSFORM YOU INTO SOMEONE YOU ARE NOT.
>
> *- Paulo Coelho*

Funerals are a vulnerable time for many people. Triggers, in the form of people/relatives, are all around you. People are hurt over the present loss and sometimes reignite dormant unforgiveness and lash out and express their anger and unresolved hurts in all sorts of ways.

Unforgiveness can be used to maintain power over another person by holding them hostage to a wrong. And this wrong may be a legitimate offense. We feel "one up" when we retain this power over the other person. However, the power you are actually holding is residing in your body, not the other person's.

Your power is energy and the unforgiving energy is trapped energy because it has nowhere to go, no way to be released. Therefore, this powerful, charged, prolonged emotional state weakens your body and immune system. (More about this in Chapter 11, **Maintain Health and Wellness.**)

I am in no way discounting your feelings, your hurts, or your wounds. However, the only person who is really affected by your unforgiveness is you. I also realize that what I am suggesting is not an easy pill to swallow, but it is a necessary one for you to be whole and free and to release the pent-up negative energy inside of you.

An essential relationship that is affected when you harbor unforgiveness is your relationship with God Almighty. God is pure love and He loves you unconditionally. Love and unforgiveness cannot occupy the same space. If someone holds bitterness in their heart, their capacity to love is diminished. Therefore, unforgiveness hinders your closeness with and prayers to God (Mark 11:25-26). I don't think people fully understand that unforgiveness is not a part of God's character.

God's word is very clear on the instructions regarding forgiveness and unforgiveness:

> *Get rid of all bitterness, rage, anger, harsh words, and slander, as well as all types of evil behavior. Instead, be kind to each other, tenderhearted, forgiving one another, just as God through Christ has forgiven you.*
> *- Ephesians 4:31-32, NLT*

He does not punish us for all our sins; he does not deal harshly with us, as we deserve.For his unfailing love toward those who fear him is as great as the height of the heavens above the earth. He has removed our sins as far from us as the east is from the west.
- Psalm 103:10-12, NLT

Whenever you stand up to pray, forgive whatever you have against anyone, so that your Father in heaven will forgive your sins. But if you do not forgive, your Father in heaven will not forgive your sins. - Mark 11:25-26, ISV

If he sins against you seven times in a day, and seven times comes back to you and says, 'I repent,' forgive him.
-L uke 17:4, NIV

The Lord our God is merciful and forgiving, even though we have rebelled against him. - Daniel 9:9, NIV

But if we confess our sins, he is faithful and just to forgive us our sins and cleanse us from everything we've done wrong. -1 John 1:9, CEB

God's word emphatically declares He will forgive you, no matter the degree of sin. In the same manner that God forgives you of your sins, be thankful for God's mercy toward you and, in turn, extend mercy to those who have wronged you.

Another cost of unforgiveness is that your spiritual development is thwarted. Your spiritual development is central to your growth in God and to your purpose, which is divine in nature. Each challenge we face in life and in our interpersonal relationships, which invariably leads to offenses, is another opportunity to grow in love.

The word of God says: *Love the Lord your God with all your heart and with all your soul and with all your mind and with all your strength.* The second is this:

> *'Love your neighbor as yourself.' There is no commandment greater than these. - Mark 12:30-31, NLT*

Your spiritual development hinges on maintaining a close love relationship with God and keeping His word. "God . . . has blessed us in Christ with every spiritual blessing in the heavenly places, just as he chose us in Christ before the foundation of the world to be holy and blameless before him in love." *(Ephesians1:3-4, NRSV)*. As we grow spiritually, our purpose will become clearer and our work will have more impact. And God promises that he will bless the work of our hands *(Deuteronomy 28:12)*. Let us stay closely connected to God and continue to grow in love and in our purpose.

The more you stay in a state of unforgiveness, the more you will attract additional situations and offenses that will need to be forgiven. Energy attracts "like" energy.

There are plenty of costs of unforgiveness. Count the costs that have already been added to your "bill" and make the smart decision to "cash-out" of unforgiveness.

BARRIERS TO UNFORGIVENESS

You may unconsciously be in survival mode–doing everything you can just to make it. And you may not even be aware of the need to divorce or detach from the emotions associated with unforgiveness (anger, bitterness, resentment, hatred). You've become accustomed to this unforgiving state. It's become a part of your identity – you and it have been going steady for as long as you can remember.

The main reason we hold on to unforgiveness is because it allows us to feel something, to identify with something or someone. The fear is that if we annihilate the pain, we will be left with nothing. We will become a no-body, a shell with no emotion, because we are afraid to be happy, joyous, and free.

Why? Because . . . what if I get hurt again? What if I open myself up and get betrayed again? So we keep the door to our hearts closed tight, sealed up, so that no air or light can enter. As a result, we're suffocating on the inside and it's cold and dark.

The barrier is the reluctance to release, detach, and give up the pain. You don't have to know "how." You just need a willingness to finally be free. Also know that when you do release the unforgiveness, you will have the freedom to create a new identity, a lasting one based on love and forgiveness.

Perhaps you are so steeped in survival mode that you are unaware of the need to forgive. In my survival mode (running from child sexual abuse), I ran so hard and fast that I never developed any feelings of resentment, hatred, or bitterness toward my perpetrator.

However, because I had the sense of control stripped from me, I lashed out in other ways, including road rage. In my road rage fits, I "fight back" by aggressively defending my territory in the lanes when merging, or if someone is "riding my tail," etc. by speeding up, slowing down, not moving over out of the fast lane–all reactionary risky actions to let the offending driver know that he/she will not be able to "get over on me." Since I have "Come Back to Myself," I am working to consciously choose not to engage in road rage.

I also suffered from clinically diagnosed depression. However, I didn't associate the road rage or the depression with my perpetrator. Once I got control of the effects of the child sexual abuse, then I could turn my attention to forgiving my perpetrator.

Something else that may be a symptom of harboring unforgiveness is racing through life without developing meaningful relationships. You may have experienced a situation in which you were offended and were subconsciously rendered non-existent. If you haven't dealt with that pain yet and forgiven the offender, you may have a difficult time being a part of a close relationship. Perhaps your unconscious reluctance or unwillingness to develop intimate relationships stems from an unrecognized association to the hurt and the need to forgive certain individuals.

Another barrier to unforgiveness is our need to feel justified when someone has wronged us. This is natural as human beings. We expect an offender to recognize the error of his ways, to come to us and apologize and possibly even beg for our forgiveness. We feel wronged and do not want to let people off easily. We believe that what he did demands restitution to the degree of the offense.

There may be some cases where restitution can be made or awarded. However, even in those cases, you are allowing someone else to hold the keys to your power and your freedom. In essence, you have handed them the keys to the prison you have built for yourself. This is way too much control and power to place in another person's hands while you wait for them to say they're sorry.

Take back the keys and let's walk through the steps of forgiveness together. Know that forgiveness is not about the other person, it's all about you.

SEVEN STEPS TO FORGIVENESS

As you take the following seven brave steps toward forgiveness, please remember to be patient with yourself and seek counseling from a qualified spiritual leader or coach as needed. Know that seven represents completion and I believe you will be completely free and whole after going through these steps.

Step 1: Decide to forgive and be free

This is the most important step. Your freedom is more important than anything in the world. Decide that forgiveness is the best thing you could ever do for yourself.

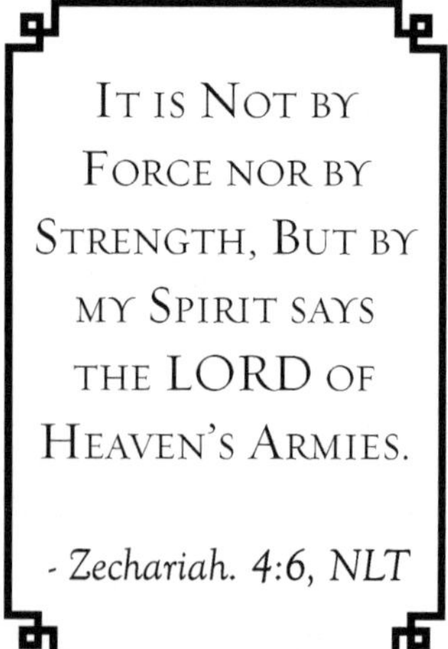

Step 2: Embrace God's word about forgiveness

God tells us to forgive others in order to be forever forgiven from our past sins and future sins. So we have to forgive anyone who has hurt us in order for us to be freely forgiven for any wrong we have done.

Being forgiven means there will never be any demand of payment for any harm caused by any offense (sin). So if we say we have forgiven our perpetrator but are still expecting anything from them (apology, payment, acknowledgement of what they did), then our forgiveness of them is not yet complete.

Step 3: Surrender the hurt and offenses to God

God is all powerful and you can give your burdens to the LORD, and he will take care of you. He will not permit the godly to slip and fall (Psalm 55:22). You can take your list of every offense and offender that we developed in the last chapter and hand them over to God.

Step 4: Come to God with an open heart and seek His Presence

Come to God with the intention to forgive everyone and everything, now and forever, of every intentional and unintentional offense.

Sit before the Lord in His Presence until you experience a complete cleansing of every ounce of unforgiveness. Seek forgiveness for yourself and your sins. You do not have to force anything.

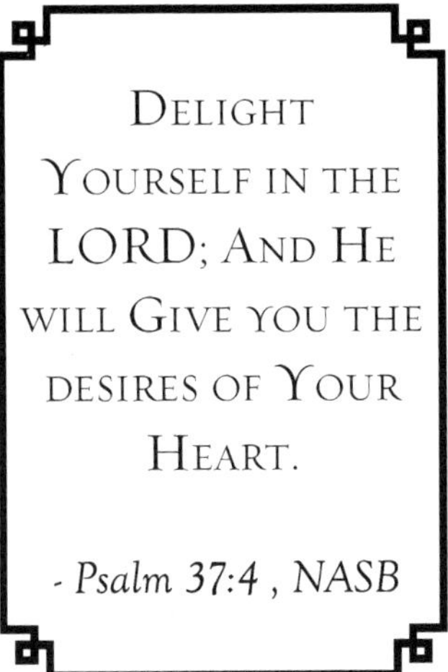

. . . it is not by force nor by strength, but by my Spirit says the LORD of Heaven's Armies. -Zechariah 4:6, NLT

You will know that you have become free when you have a sense of calm and a peace about the people and situations.

Step 5: Trust that God will honor the desire of your heart to forgive

Trust that God will do the inner work that only His Holy Spirit can do through your open heart. Ask God to soften your heart so His love can penetrate your heart and you can forgive.

Delight yourself in the LORD; And He will give you the desires of your heart. - Psalm 37:4, NASB

Trust in the LORD with all your heart And do not lean on your own understanding. - Proverbs 3:5, ESV

You don't have to understand the "how." The work belongs to the Lord.

Step 6: Pray for your offender

Then commit to pray for the well-being of your offender.

But I say to you, Love your enemies, bless them that curse you, do good to them that hate you, and pray for them which spitefully use you, and persecute you.
- Matthew 5:44, AKJV

I completely understand that this commandment is a hard one to do. But God will not tell us to do something that was not for our highest good. This step will undoubtedly be one of your most challenging steps in this seven-step process. I encourage you to trust God and stay connected to God's love during this step. Do only what you can with where you are. You can also seek assistance for this step as well.

Step 7: Walk in your new freedom with thanksgiving and renew your commitment to maintain a forgiving heart

Rejoice with thanksgiving that you been faithful to the word of God concerning forgiveness and God has been faithful to His word.

For he has rescued us from the kingdom of darkness and transferred us into the Kingdom of his dear Son, who purchased our freedom and forgave our sins.
- Colossians 1:13-14, NLT

A wonderful, miraculous divine experience has occurred. Never discount your experience and the power of it.

Give thanks in everything, for this is God's will for you in Christ Jesus. - 1 Thessalonians 5:18, HCSB

Ask God to forgive you of your sins daily and go forward from this point with an open heart willing to forgive.

THE BENEFITS OF BEING FREED-UP

Once you get freed-up by forgiving everyone and everything associated with your past hurt, you will invariably be exposed to new challenges that will test your resolve to stay freed-up. Your job is to renew your mind daily. Overdose with love and more love. No one ever died from too much love. Bathe and bask in God's love, forgiveness, and unconditional acceptance of you every day. Elevate your awareness of your new way of being completely freed-up.

A side benefit of being freed-up is that you will attract at your new level, at your new awareness and consciousness. Love attracts. It attracts health, wealth, love, and harmony. If there is excess weight, I would not be surprised if the weight begins to shed itself from your elevated presence.

Remember, you have been self-medicating to suppress your pain. Now you are no longer bogged down with trapped energy in your cells; it has been released. Your walk should be lighter, your strides longer and more purposeful. And you will have more energy to pursue your purpose, to go after your heart's desire.

Maintain a heart ready to forgive. Forgiveness is an ongoing process. As long as there are humans, there will be someone something to forgive. Keep your heart full of God's love and not only will certain transgressions not even register with you but, if they do, you will have a greater capacity to forgive and stay whole and free.

You have participated in a miraculous work. You have become freed-up. Now you are ready to express more of the real you.

Next, let's explore what really matters to you as we turn to the next section and learn how to Own Your Greatness.

AFFIRMATION

I forgive everyone and everything, now and forever, of both intentional and unintentional offenses, and my soul is whole and free.

TIPS AND STRATEGIES TO FORGIVENESS

- Answer the call of your soul to be free and forgive.
- Count the costs of unforgiveness concerning your spiritual and physical health, relationships, and spiritual development.
- Overcome the resistance to forgiveness by identifying the barriers to forgiveness that affect you.
- Go through the seven-step process for forgiveness. Be patient and expect complete freedom.

- Don't force forgiveness; depend and trust God to do the inner work.

- Pray for the well-being of your offenders, when you are ready.

- Give thanks and rejoice in your new freedom.

- Ask God to show you areas where you sin and ask for forgiveness daily.

- Keep no record of wrongs going forward.

- Keep an open heart for forgiveness.

- Accept yourself and accept others as they are. Love them more.

To err is human,
to forgive is divine.

- Alexander Pope

SECTION 2

Own Your Greatness

CHAPTER FIVE

DANCE WITH YOUR SOUL

Feel the beat in your heart, and dance the beat.
- Giavanni Olivia DeGuzman

In the first section, you spent time becoming freed-up. So you're freed-up, now what?

Now that the fog has lifted from past hurts, wounds and unforgiveness, your deepest passion has a chance to resurface. You can begin the process to get back in touch with the things, events, and people that make your soul dance. Let's get started.

GO AFTER WHAT YOU REALLY WANT

As I shared in my story, the child sexual abuse began when I was nine years old. While it affected me greatly, during that time I did not tell anyone about the abuse and essentially went on living my life as normally as I could.

There was something else that started when I was nine years old–something I now believe probably helped keep my sanity during that tragic year. I started teaching.

My classroom was in my grandparent's basement on the weekends. Card tables served as my students' desks. I found some hardcover textbooks that seemed to be there just for me. I put a whiteboard between two chairs and that served as my chalkboard. A table, which served as my desk, was in front of my students' desks. I gave full lessons, very matter of factly. Somehow, even at nine years old, I instinctually knew my students needed a break, so I released them for about 10 minutes or so.

My students? Why, they were my two brothers (one older and one younger) and my baby sister. During "recess" they raced upstairs for dear life, hoping to be rescued by my grandparents. My grandmother would hand out popsicles. My older brother would cozy up to my Grandfather and quietly ask: "Do we have to go back down there?" What do you think my grandfather said? "Yes, you do." Yes! I would think to myself with a hand gesture like I had just aced Serena Williams in tennis. I had my students back and all was well with my world–at least for the weekend.

Well, I continued to teach school with my relenting siblings, which led to me tutoring other students in elementary school and high school. I believe I became interested in boys in middle school–which accounts for the fact I had no time for tutoring during those years.

When the time came for me to apply for college, I only applied to two local universities, because I didn't want to leave my boyfriend. I applied for a major in education at both universities. However, between the time I applied and before I started classes in the fall, I changed my major to business.

At that time, there was a lot of press about teaching being such a demanding field. Too much homework to grade each night, and all those unruly students and their uncooperative parents. Well, that was all I needed to hear. And I didn't have anyone to counter those reports. My rationale was I would go into business, make a lot of money, and when I retired, I would teach.

Here's the lesson: my soul danced with teaching and education from the time I was nine years old, when I essentially started my "teaching career." I allowed external forces (e.g., media) to shape my perception and alter my trajectory. Fortunately, I have always been in professional positions where I was able to give workshops and training, which continued to fuel what my soul knows it wants. However, I feel like I never fully engaged in the field for what I wanted to do and what I was good at doing. While everything works together for one's good (Romans 8:28), I believe I would have been further along in my professional career in education had I pursued teaching initially.

> KNOW AT THE CENTER OF YOUR BEING, YOU HAVE THE ANSWER, YOU KNOW WHO YOU ARE AND YOU KNOW WHAT YOU WANT.
>
> *- Lao Tzu*

There's a hidden part of you that knows what it wants. It's been there since the very beginning. The confident, unquestioning child doesn't ask for permission, doesn't second-guess their knowing, she just goes after whatever emanates from her heart and soul.

One day my son asked me and his little sister for some quick instructions for a dance our family was heading to later that night. My daughter replied without hesitation: "Feel the beat in your heart, and dance the beat." I have never heard such a profound statement, especially coming from a six-year-old. But she clearly is free, unrestricted, and "knows her way." As I said in the Introduction, I wish I could capture her essence and bottle it, because most of us start here but venture so far away from our true knowing and our true selves–like I did with teaching.

Les Brown is a world-class motivational speaker and I had the privilege of sharing the stage with him during a speaking engagement where I got to share my story. One of Les Brown's most famous quotes is, *"You become what you are."* I know that is true in my story. And now it's time to explore and revisit what it is you truly want for yourself.

So let's go through some exercises to help you come back to yourself and get back in touch with the real you.

WDYWFY, FR!

Now that we are freed-up and letting go of everything that's keeping us from being what we were created to be, we can dream again, revisit what we really want, and redesign our life.

When I was a financial planner, I would start a financial session with a new client with the same question, WDYWFY?, which stands for "what do you want for yourself?" Now that I teach young people this same process, I have added the letters, "FR" at the end. WDYWFY, FR?, which stands for "what do you want for yourself, for real?"

There's no time for playing small. Remove the filters and just say what you want. Don't worry about how it sounds, how old you are, your educational background, your weight, or any other thing outside of your inner knowing and desire. Don't worry about whether you know how to do what it is you say you really want to do. The process follows desire, not the other way around.

Here are a few questions to help you get started:

- If I asked you to paint a picture of what you want, what would it look like?

- If you had limited time left on earth, what would you say you have to accomplish before that time was up?
- What do you want to achieve in your lifetime?
- How would your true self explain what you want to a magical genie who could grant your every spoken wish?
- What does it look like and feel like to have achieved your WDYWFY, FR?
- How would you carry yourself if you were living out your true desire?
- Who would be in your new circle? Who are your new associates?

The most important take-away here is to know that you don't have to have the money, the time, or the resources right now to actually go after what you really want. First of all you need to be brave enough and bold enough to state what you want. That's all you need to do in this moment.

Start to imagine this picture of the new you every morning and every night. What you are doing is re-envisioning yourself, your true self. You'll become so comfortable with this image that you will soon begin to take on the characteristics naturally and you'll start to engage in activities that are in alignment with this new image of yourself.

Later in life, I discovered that I love to dance, specifically ballroom dancing and Latin Hustle. One year my husband and I gave a Valentine's party. This party was the way for me to fulfill my desire to dance since my husband and I rarely went dancing.

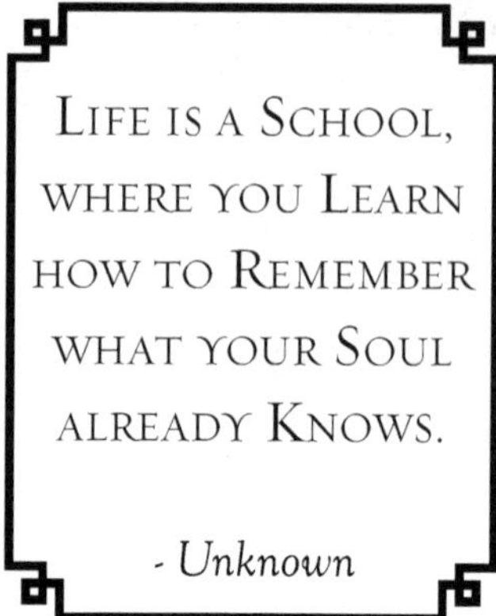

We hired dance instructors to teach all the attendees how to do ballroom dances, the hustle, and salsa. I was instantly hooked. Even with my very first lesson, I was in my element. It actually came very naturally for me.

I continued to take dance lessons, group dance lessons that is, until I became impatient with the pace. Eventually I was able to start private lessons because my dance partner is a dance instructor. He and I are now practicing for competition.

Whatever feeds your soul, do it. Make time for it and take time for it. Even if it is for pure enjoyment, like gardening or baking or art or competitive ballroom dancing. Do what makes you happy. There are certain people and activities that add life to our life. When we incorporate them into our life, we begin to feel at a deeper level. Make a decision to prioritize these opportunities in order to feel more, to express more of who you really are.

BARRIERS TO DANCING WITH YOUR SOUL

Societal Expectations

Why do we hesitate to let go and do what we feel? Well, society has a glaring eye that reminds us of our place in life. Do you know of the story of King David, who danced in the streets as the ark of the covenant of the Lord was entering the city?

Well, his royal wife, Michal, reminded David of his esteemed place in the courts of royalty and that King David should be certain to remember that he was the King and not some commoner, dancing about in the street.

> Once in a while It really hits People that they Don't have to Experience the world in the Way they Have been told.
>
> - *Alan Keightley*

As the ark of the covenant of the LORD was entering the City of David, Michal daughter of Saul, watched from a window. And when she saw King David dancing and celebrating, she despised him in her heart. - 1 Chronicles 15:29, NIV

Fortunately, his wife's reproach did not cause King David to shrink back and focus on the dignity of his kingship. He was elated and danced to express his joyous triumph.

Conformity

Our educational system is designed to maintain the status quo. Very few members of society move beyond the rigid structure that goes something like this: graduate from high school, go to college and/or get a job, get married, buy a house, have kids, buy a bigger house, obtain a bigger mortgage, buy fancier cars, take vacations, get promoted, repeat and retire. Most Americans make enough money to have a comfortable lifestyle, pay their bills, and hopefully save enough to send their kids to college, take care of their parents and make it through retirement. This scenario is respectful and practical.

Yet over 70% of Americans are doing work that does not feed their souls and are "not engaged" or "actively disengaged" from their work.[1]

Now consider this scenario, a college student leaves college during his first semester to go to New York to pursue his soul's passion of acting, singing and dancing. There is no structure or formula. He follows his passion and trusts his inner knowing that the right opportunity will present itself. He struggles and has to wait tables, but he never gives up until he makes it big.

I recently attended an event where I heard a story about the actors Wesley Snipes and Laurence Fishburne. A presenter at the event shared that these two men ate bologna sandwiches and worked menial jobs while going on audition after audition until they both eventually got their big breaks. They supported each other during the down times and provided encouragement along the way. I also believe they each possessed a desire to "dance with their soul" no matter what.

When I was a founding director of an alumni career center of a Big Ten University, I counseled hundreds of alumni who sought counseling because they had achieved a level of success in their chosen career field, but were unfulfilled and often only going through the motions for a paycheck needed to maintain their lifestyle. In essence they were wearing golden handcuffs – locked in a good job for financial security and to maintain their lifestyle.

These alumni would love to have had a "do-over." They definitely would have pursued a field of study that made their souls dance. However, for the vast majority of them, they're stuck because of their bills. Sometimes these alumni find volunteer opportunities that fulfill their passion or they wait until their retirement when they can have a second career and support themselves on the reduced income. But the longing is always there.

Whether you go into business for yourself, find part-time employment, seek out volunteer or civic opportunities, it is important to go after what you want for yourself.

Respectability

Now, there may be some activities that we shy away from because it will make us look like we're not acting our age or like we're going through a middle-age crisis. For example, as I shared a few paragraphs back, I discovered that I love to dance. And now my dance partner and I are practicing for competition.

One of the first questions I'm asked when I'm out dancing without my husband is, "Does your husband dance?" This is a kind way of asking, "Your husband allows you to dance with other men?" Or, "Wouldn't it be more respectful if your husband learned how to dance so he could dance with you?"

I am very conciliatory in my response and downplay their veiled questions. However, I quickly got to a point where I no longer cared about who was watching me dance (without my husband) or the manner in which I danced. I am a dancer! And most of the men that I dance with (at our competition level) are dancers, too! So you may have to turn a blind eye to external glares and nosy questions.

Do you know why people question your actions that are outside of their status quo? Because they don't have the courage to do it, so it's hard for them to understand how you can do it without second-guessing yourself. They want to be sure you know what you're doing – dancing with other men.

Practicality

A very good friend of mine gave up a six-figure salary to follow her passion to help young girls who are at risk for not completing high school or attending college. She created an organization called Girls Group that provides the mentorship and programming to give these young women windows of opportunities for a better life and an education.

My friend received "talks" from well-meaning corporate friends and family: "Do you know what you're doing? Do you even know how to relate to the girls you're trying to help? After all, you're white and they're black." Her organization is now in its 12th year. My friend still doesn't take a salary and is having a significant impact on middle, high school and college girls' lives.

We don't want to be seen as different and there are very few other people "dancing with their souls." So we don't have the support to counter the "friendly assaults" on our dreams.

I attended a girl's empowerment conference where a well-known magazine editor gave the keynote address. She told the audience that we could literally do anything we wanted. After her talk, I approached her and told her of my dream to start a school for girls. Do you know what the first words out of her mouth were? "You can't do that." Wow! I couldn't believe what I was hearing.

> TRADITION BECOMES OUR SECURITY, AND WHEN THE MIND IS SECURE IT IS IN DECAY.
>
> *- Krishnamurti*

This prominent editor had just finished telling me and the entire audience that we could do anything. But when I shared my dream, suddenly I couldn't do that. Who was I to dare to start a school for girls? My first school will open in 2017. This first school will not be an all-girls school, but the all-girls school will open shortly thereafter.

When you know what you want, realize that other people will try to "bring you to your senses" because you are leaving mediocrity and stability. You are taking a risk that many individuals don't have the courage to take. They don't have the vision to see what you can see. That is also why you have to "see" it clearly and definitively.

> EVERYTHING YOU WANT IS ON THE OTHER SIDE OF FEAR.
>
> *- Jack Canfield*

They would rather play it safe and secure. And they often participate in activities and work at jobs that have no soul value or meaning to them. And they grow older and older.

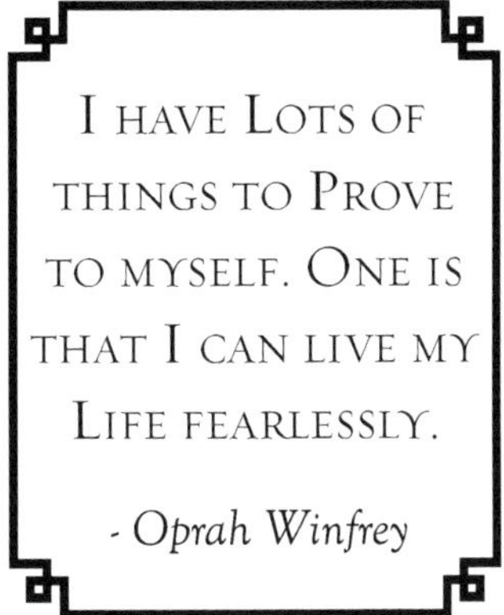

Fear

Les Brown said, "Too many of us are not living our dreams because we are living our fears." Probably the chief reason we don't go after what we truly desire is out of fear. We fear the unknown, the isolation, the financial uncertainly, the loss of loved ones. You can fill in the rest.

I would like to say to you that success is on the other side of fear. You will never know your true potential by staying on the shore where it is safe and solid.

Fear is a natural part of the process of becoming successful. Our internal fear barometer is there to protect us from potentially harmful situations. An internal alarm usually goes off when we are entering a dangerous situation. This served us well in the age of the dinosaurs. However, today we are not typically faced with dangerous situations that pertain to our dreams.

No one will hurt you if you leave college to pursue your dream. If you decide to quit your job to pursue your dream, you will not be arrested. Override your fears by confronting them and exploring the worst possible outcome. Decide how likely it would be if your fear were to come true. If there is a high probability that the thing you fear will not come true, then go after your dreams.

Also know that if your fear does come true (you lose money, you fail, you succeed, you lose the love of a loved one), you will live and you will be able to recover. Therefore, there is nothing to prevent you from going after your dreams. Fear is part of the process of accomplishing your goals. You must acknowledge it while continuing to work through it until you've reached your goal. Enlist those around you to support you. There are people like me who are happy to help you through this process. It's easier than you think.

Commit to Dancing With Your Soul

Now it is time to fully commit to what you really want. Don't deny yourself what you want. (I am assuming that what you want doesn't infringe upon someone's personal property or marital vows.)

Let's stop pretending and lying to ourselves that our wants don't have meaning and value. If you want to make a difference in the world, you have to commit to what you say it is you want and then go after it. And remember, you don't have to know the "how."

Think of your integrity. Value yourself enough to keep your word to yourself. If you say you are going to start a girls' school, then do it. If you want to write a book, then do it.

One day I asked a friend for some start-up funds for my girls' school. He told me that I was not committed. I honestly couldn't believe that he "called me out" in that way, but he was right. At the time, I wasn't "sold out," 100% determined that, no matter what, I was going to start the girls' school. He is very perceptive.

That lesson has stayed with me. Now I truly know what I want and I'm going after it with everything I've got. Even though you don't have all the answers, people will help you once you commit to the vision. And, yes, he and his wife later gave me the start-up funds.

Once you become committed, it's not difficult for others to believe in your vision. One day at a dinner event, I described my vision of a girls' school to an individual who sat next to me. She said that I gave her chill bumps because I spoke with such vividness, assurance, and conviction.

So many people are not committed to their dreams. They don't stand for anything. They're not looking to make a difference. That may be okay for them, but you would not be reading this book if that were you. You are looking to make a difference. You want to achieve what it is you say you want. You're tired of playing small to make others feel comfortable. You are freed-up and ready to declare your wants and desires and make a commitment that, no matter what, you will achieve it.

AFFIRMATION

I honor my inner knowing and desire of what I want for myself, for real. I go after it no matter what and I feel alive.

TIPS AND STRATEGIES TO DANCE WITH YOUR SOUL

- Take the time to re-imagine what you really want for yourself and feel how you would feel if you were living your dream.
- Do more of what makes your soul dance!
- Enlist a dream-team who will support your vision and encourage you when you begin to question yourself and your abilities. (More on this in Chapter 8.)
- Turn a blind eye and ear to societal expectations for normalcy and respectability.

- Be committed to what you really want for yourself. If you are not committed, you may succumb to the "friendly assaults" on your dreams.

- Go after your dream even if you don't know the "how." You already have everything inside of you to get started: desire. Once you put the ball in motion, you will discover the "how."

If you don't build your dream, someone will hire you to help build theirs.

-Tony A. Gaskins Jr.

CHAPTER SIX

CREATE YOUR VISION, MISSION AND VALUES

Create the highest, grandest vision possible for your life because you become what you believe. - Oprah Winfrey

You're doing great! You're dancing with your soul and beginning to live a freed-up life. Now it's time to clarify where you're headed.

An empire is created from someone's vision. Why don't we have a vision for ourselves? Who takes the time to write out the "highest, grandest vision possible" for their life? Who knows how to? Instead, most of us have been drafted to advance someone else's vision.

Now you have the opportunity and the time to create your vision for you. You will do this by defining your vision and then daily decreeing and delivering your mission. Your vision and mission will be in alignment with your values, which are emanating from your new level of freedom and self-awareness.

To help you get started, I want you to think about the #1 reason for your existence. Why are you here? What is your purpose for being here? What do you truly stand for? What is one word that defines the essence of who you are?

Here are some examples of what I'm talking about (according to my perception):

- Martin Luther King: Justice
- Tiger Woods: Golf
- President Barack Obama: Change
- Oprah Winfrey: Transformation
- Michael Jordan: Basketball
- Bill Gates: Transformation
- Jesus: Love

> LET GO THE THINGS IN WHICH YOU ARE IN DOUBT FOR THE THINGS IN WHICH THERE IS NO DOUBT.
>
> *- Mohammed*

When you remove others' expectations, confront your fears and doubts, and embrace who you truly are, then you can pursue your purpose with confidence and self-assuredness. Remember in a previous chapter I shared with you that I wanted to be a teacher from the age of nine? I also shared that I was actually teaching my brothers and sister. No one gave me permission to teach, no one handed me a teaching certificate and interviewed me. I was doing what I was born to do. This is the place where I would like you to reconnect with.

I don't necessarily want to be a teacher right now in my professional trajectory, but the essence of who I am is an educator. I teach. I guess I am teaching right now through this book. You are unique and have treasures within you. Let's help you get crystal clear about who you are and why you exist.

> I KNOW WHERE I'M GOING AND I KNOW THE TRUTH, AND I DON'T HAVE TO BE WHAT YOU WANT ME TO BE. I'M FREE TO BE WHAT I WANT.
>
> *- Muhammed Ali*

DEFINE YOUR WHY

Let's start with a reflectionary view of why you exist, why you do what you do. I'm not talking about reflecting on what or how you do what you do, but why you do what you do.

Simon Sinek is a TED speaker whose first TEDx talk, *"How Great Leaders Inspire Action,"* has been ranked the third most watched TED Talk video. Simon believes the most innovative and successful people and companies lead from the inside out. That is, they think, act, and communicate their beliefs to others from the inside out.[1]

There are very few leaders who operate this way. The vast majority of leaders and companies operate from the outside in. They position themselves to sell and communicate what they do. A few leaders sell and communicate how they do what they do. But the most innovative and successful leaders sell and communicate their why.

From this moment on, you are going to Define, Declare, and Daily Deliver your belief of your Why so that every decision you make is in alignment with your Why. Do you realize that every decision you have ever made has resulted in your life being as it is right now?

For example, here is a snippet of why I am writing this book.

I believe women are the most beautiful of all God's creation. He endowed us with grace and beauty. From this place, we can do anything we truly desire to do. But so many of us are stuck, oppressed, and underutilizing our God-given potential. Based on this belief, I want women and girls to know their power, strength, and beauty and operate from the essence of their being to accomplish great things, whatever that is for them.

Now it's your turn. Define your why. Take a moment and think about your why. Spend some time journaling your answer to these questions:

Why do I exist?
What do I want?
Why is this important to me?

DECREE YOUR WHY DAILY

You will decree a thing and it will be established for you. And light will shine on your ways. - Job 22:28, NASB

It's important that you decree, another word could be declare, your why–and how you will carry out your why–out loud every day. When you saturate your subconscious with your desire, combined with emotion and conviction, the Universe will see that it is established for you. But there has to be enough energy generated from your being so the Universe can pick up the "signal" to what it is you're attempting to accomplish.

Here is my daily decree:

To be recognized as a world-class educational leader who builds schools for girls to thrive on their own terms and accomplish their life's mission. I transform women's lives through my speaking and coaching practice. I operate from an essence of freedom and love.

Now let's define how you will position yourself in life and the marketplace to act on and communicate your why.

Your why should be reflected in the job you have. For example, don't just work for a paycheck. If you're going to work for a person or a company, then look at their mission. Does it align with your why? If it doesn't, you are simply working for a paycheck. I know we have all worked to pay the bills and put food on the table. However, you are now freed-up. From this state, never compromise or relinquish your freedom. Remember, every decision you have made has resulted in your life today. Make new decisions based on your why.

> AND, WHEN YOU WANT SOMETHING, ALL THE UNIVERSE CONSPIRES IN HELPING YOU TO ACHIEVE IT.
>
> *- Paulo Coelho*

One time I interviewed for a position. My initial reaction to the posting was not to apply. But then two trusted advisors independently encouraged me to apply, so I did. I made it through the second round of interviews. The second interview lasted all day and I met with everyone, including the dean of the school.

In the meeting with the dean, I was asked why I wanted to work for that particular school. I definitively told her that, while I believed in the mission of the school, I would not be the ideal spokesperson for the school. The position did inherently embody the role of spokesperson, because it was the leader of a unit that recruited prospective students and engaged current students and alumni.

I could hear myself respond with authority that I could do the job but I was not the "spokesperson." My why certainly did not align with her why or the school's why. After meeting with the team, who seemed to be diametrically opposed to everything on the Dean's agenda, I knew this was not the position for me. I withdrew my application the next day.

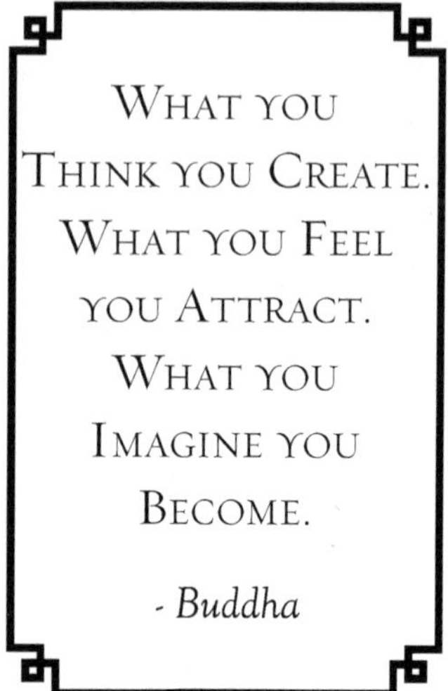

Don't give your time and energy to causes, jobs, or relationships that are not aligned with your why or to ones that cannot advance your why and that you cannot collaborate with. From your freed-up self, be selective with your time and energy. Don't give it away so freely. Think, act, and communicate from your why.

What about your relationships? You need to choose to spend more time with people who share your why–so when joined together, you both can make the other's why stronger and better. Can you see the power in aligning yourself with people who are like-minded? Can you see the passion, synergy, and energy combining into something great?

CREATE THE LIFE YOU WANT

How will you think, act and communicate your why? Here are three tools to help you create and govern your why–to help you create the life you want.

1. Vision
2. Mission
3. Values

Determine Your Vision

VISION-VISIONARY

First, think about your why daily. Renew your mind daily by reviewing your why statement every morning and every night so it can get into your subconscious. Very few people have a conscious-level explicit vision for themselves. Can you incorporate your why into a written vision statement?

Think of vision in terms of a vision-ary. Someone who envisions what is possible. For whom? For what? How do you envision your life? Your family? Your community? The world in which you live? What is most important to you? What makes you angry? What makes you sad? Who do you hurt for? Who does your heart scream out for? Who do you have the most compassion for?

One example of a visionary that we are all familiar with is Mother Teresa. She devoted her life to the "poorest among the poor." She had a vision to serve human beings who were destitute and dejected with dignity and love. Mother Teresa received the Nobel Peace Prize in 1979 and she was beatified as "Blessed Teresa of Calcutta." As the head of Missionaries of Charity, she inspired over 4,000 religious sisters to adopt her vision, creating 610 foundations in 123 countries.[2]

A vision is what you see that others don't. You see what is possible and you see the potential.

What is the change that you want to create for the future? What is the difference you are dying to make? Can you align with a person or an organization that is already envisioning such a new future? This is why you should not just work for anyone. If you are going to pursue a career, make sure to give thought to why.

A vision consists of a statement that is somewhere beyond where you are right now. It can be defined as a stretch goal–one you will reach five, ten, twenty years from now. It describes what you ultimately want to achieve, how you want to live, what you want to have, and what differentiates you from anyone else.

Your vision should guide your day-to-day decisions. Your vision is something that you feel emotionally and want to have happen in a way that is different from someone else. The way I feel about young girls standing up for themselves and owning their own power will be to a different degree than you. Whatever it is that you feel with emotion, that ignites something on the inside of you, pay attention to that. I remember observing a second grade classroom. My heart melted because the kids were so adorable and practically empty vessels, so hungry for knowledge and connection.

Review your why and write a 1-2 sentence vision statement that answers these questions:

What would the world look like if you were doing everything you thought you could be doing and you had all the resources you needed?

What does the end result look like?

Define Your Mission

MISSION - MISSIONARY

Think about your mission as something you were born to do, the overall core purpose for your life. What you aim to do for your life's work. Consider how you want to be remembered. (See chapter on Leave an Impact and a Legacy.) What distinguishes your mission from someone else's?

Your mission is defined as how you will carry out your vision; what you are doing in the present to accomplish your future state–your vision. Think of a mission-ary, someone who carries out the work of the vision, putting the vision into practice. Think of mission accomplished.

Talk about your mission in the context of your why. You inspire others from your vision and not the how-to of your mission. Your mission communicates how you will carry out your vision.

Who does your mission benefit?

Here is an example of my mission:

To educate and inspire women and girls to remove internal barriers, become freed-up, own and operate in their greatness through engaging workshops, informative books, and life-transformative coaching in order to fulfill their purpose.

Take some time to start writing out your Mission.

Answer these questions:

What do you do?

How do you do it?

Who does it benefit?

What value do you bring?

REFINE YOUR VALUES

Values represent everything that governs our behaviors internally and externally. Most people are not in touch with their values. Yet, "Values are your heart's deepest desire for how you want to behave as a human being."[3] They can also be described as your internal beliefs of how you desire to live.

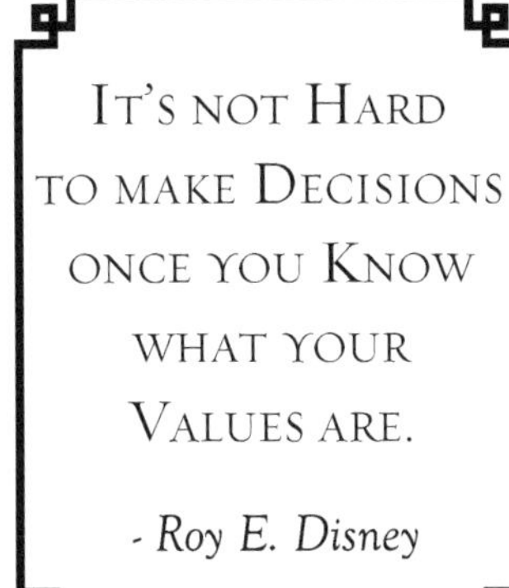

Values define what you will stand for. Your values are your guideposts to make sure you are making decisions that are congruent to the future you are trying to create through your vision. Values are the core essence of who you really are.

As it relates to your mission, values are about how you are going to behave or act in carrying out your mission.

Since you've done the inner work described in Part 1 of this book, I think it's a good time to redefine your values based on being freed-up. What are your essential beliefs about what really matters to you? Here is a partial list of values for you to consider:

- Honesty
- Acceptance
- Love
- Commitment
- Well-being
- Intimacy
- Integrity
- Fun-loving
- Health-conscious
- Intellectual
- Ambitious

I've included in the Resources the link to The Happiness Trap where you can find an exhaustive list of values and how to rank their importance to you. You will find 60 values to get you started in the right direction. You job is to choose six of them, rank them in order of importance to you, and start to integrate your values into how you carry out your mission.

I highly recommend that you write out your values on an index card and review them daily so you can become conscious of your values and make decisions that are in alignment with them. Living out your values is not predicated on external circumstances. That is why your values have to become a part of the very fabric of your being, so there is no hesitancy in knowing what you truly stand for.

MISSION INTEGRATION

So how are you going to incorporate your vision, mission and values into your new freed-up life? You're going to behave as if your vision is happening right now, in the present. You can do this by making sure every life decision reflects your vision, mission, and values. Only do actions that are "mission-aligned" (i.e., support the intent of your mission). It is through our "moment-to-moment decisions" that we move closer to fulfilling our mission and changing lives.[4]

In order to ensure that your decisions incorporate your vision, mission, and values, it is very important to read your three decrees (Vision/Mission/Values) out loud every day. If you want to really integrate and know your vision, mission, and values, take time to write them out daily, preferably at the beginning of the day.

The reason we don't live by our values, which govern our behavior, is because we are not mindful of our values. In order to be strategic in living your life, you will need to develop a strategic mindset to know and live out your vision, mission, and values daily.

How about becoming the Director of Mission Integration for your why? Believe it or not, I didn't invent this title. It actually exists.

Here is some language that comes directly from a job posting for a Director of Mission Integration:

"Commitment to the mission and values of the organization, knowledge and experience in addressing contemporary health care delivery systems and clinical and organizational ethical issues facing the field, the ability to inspire and motivate others to be committed to the organization's mission, values, vision, and goals, adult learning skills, and knowledge of and commitment to the community benefit ministry. Additionally, must be spiritually grounded and pursuing a regular spiritual practice."[5]

You have to be committed to your vision, mission, and values; promoting and integrating them into all aspects of your life. There is an interesting phenomenon that occurs once you become clear of your vision, mission, and values: Other people are attracted to your radiating energy. This is the reason you don't have to be overly concerned with how you are going to implement your vision. Your chief role is to define and decree your vision. The way will be established as you commit to your why.

On a regular basis, challenge the assumption that you are operating from your freed-up new state of being. Are you really making all of your decisions based on your vision? Modify your statements as you continue to grow in your freedom.

Know that there is no limit to your growth, therefore, as you continue your growth trajectory, over the long-term, you will also outgrow the vision you have developed as of this writing. Therefore, you will need to reflect and possibly rewrite your vision and mission statements. Your core values should be pretty constant, although there could be some increased enlightenment that may deepen and expand your values.

The world needs what you have to offer and you will be the best champion of your vision. Think about how much time and energy you have expended on carrying out someone else's vision by working on their mission. Consider shifting your mindset and making a steadfast commitment to advancing your mission. Someone is waiting for you to fulfill it.

AFFIRMATION

My vision is compellingly clear. I make moment-to-moment decisions to advance my vision and change lives.

TIPS AND STRATEGIES TO CREATE YOUR VISION, MISSION AND VALUES

- Know that without a vision, the people perish (Proverbs 29:18). Your vision will save lives and enhance the quality of your life.
- Spend some quality time digging deeper into your why.
- Write out your vision, mission, and values statements. Decree and declare your statements daily.
- Create a Vision Board (cut out images from magazines that speak to you and the accomplishment of your vision). Look at your vision board daily and internalize a feeling of accomplishment from the images.
- Give thanks and express gratitude as if your vision and mission are accomplished.
- Share your vision with others. Everyone should know what's most important to you.
- Live your values regardless of external circumstances.

How do you know if your mission in life is finished? If you are still alive, it isn't.

-Richard Bach

CHAPTER SEVEN

DEVELOP YOUR POWER, PRESENCE AND VOICE

If you see a woman that has everything going for herself and you are not ready to add value to her life . . . just admire her from afar. PLEASE don't interrupt greatness. - Unknown

You've created your vision, mission and values, now think about the person you want to become.

Would you rather walk in your purpose timidly, unsure of yourself, hesitantly? Or would you rather walk in your purpose with boldness, confidence, and assuredness, owning your power, presence and voice, from the greatest expression of you?

> IF YOU WANT TO ACHIEVE GREATNESS, STOP ASKING FOR PERMISSION.
>
> *- Philosiblog*

Of course, we all vote for the latter. You can choose to own your greatness with self-assuredness and the confidence to attract others to your cause and your mission and impact lives in the process. And you don't need anyone's permission or approval.

Rise up, my sister, and harness all the gifts and power on the inside of you and attach yourself to your greatness.

DEFINE THE GREATEST EXPRESSION OF YOU

Imagine living from the greatest expression of yourself. The greatest expression of you comes from a creative space of being freed-up. It emanates from a place of love–love of God, yourself, and your neighbor.

Imagine you are on the highest cliff in the world. You take a leap up and out, arms stretched wide, smiling and beaming, feeling a lightness because there is nothing holding you back–no weight, no confusion–just beauty, peace, clarity, and joy. You soar with power, dignity, and strength. This is one image to think about as you create your best self.

I want you to use your creative, freed-up mind to imagine what the greatest expression of yourself looks like. Take some time and write down the answers to the following questions and anything else that comes to mind. You're doing great. Grab a cup of tea, settle in, and spend some time journaling your answers.

How do you feel operating from this expression?
How do you impact the world?
What problems do you solve?
Who would benefit from the greatest expression of you?

BEING CONSCIOUS OF THE GREATEST EXPRESSION OF YOU

Now that you've defined the greatest expression of yourself, it's time for you to own it. You have to be it, walk it, talk it, and live it out. There is no separation between your greatest expression of you and your everyday you. You are whole and you are one with God. Therefore, you have great power and presence.

Where you may feel a disconnect or dissonance is in your level of awareness of your greatest expression of you. That is, you have to be cognizant and realize this expression of yourself. If you do not hold a conscious awareness of this image and experience the resulting feelings associated with it, it is hard for it to "take hold." Let this image saturate your mind; let the emotions flood your being, until you seemingly merge into the greatest expression of you, effortlessly. You have become your greatest expression.

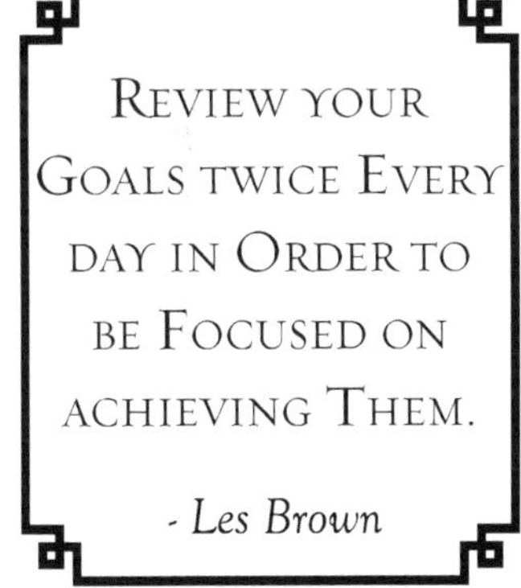

I am so glad you're reading this book. So many people are operating just as they are—not from their creative self but from their self-existing, unexamined self. However, you—oh great woman of God—you are now aware of and operating from your creative self. Not the old, false version of you, but the whole, complete, loving, healed version of you. Rejoice!

Every day you will need to review your definition of the greatest expression of you.

Do not be conformed to this world, but continuously be transformed by the renewing of your mind so that you may be able to determine what God's will is–what is proper, pleasing, and perfect. - Romans 12:2, ISV

The word of God says to "continuously" be transformed by the renewing of your mind. It will not be enough to just do the exercise of defining your greatness. You now have to continuously review it over and over again through repetition, repetition, repetition. For now, commit to reading your definition every morning and every night, at a minimum. Internalize and feel the emotions associated with imagining the greatest expression of you.

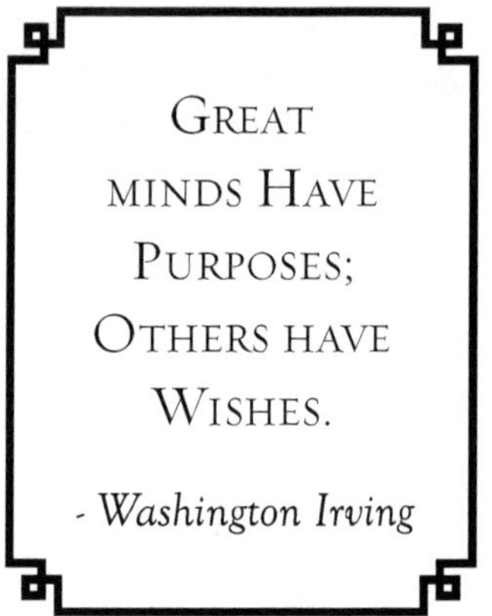

MASTERY OF YOUR GREATEST EXPRESSION

The destination called mastery is on a road called repetition. -Jeff Shore

When we think of mastery, we usually think of learning some facts and we often think of a school setting with students. I would like to expand your thinking here and propose that you need to master you and the definition of your greatness.

Another name for this type of work is called personal mastery and it is a process, not a one and done event. It takes dedicated effort and patience to truly master you.

We did quite a bit of work in the last chapter creating your vision, mission, and values. Now we are going to use this work (i.e., your vision, mission and values) as a foundation for personal mastery of the greatest expression of you. In Peter Senge's 1990 authoritative book, *The Fifth Discipline,* he describes personal mastery as the inner work we do to see clearly the best leader we can be and work towards that picture with diligence, determination, and focus.[1]

I would like to expand on the reference to being the best leader (leader of yourself) to also include the highest level of you. Personal mastery is about creating a desired future of how you want to be in the world and then moving toward it. For example, I want to be spiritually enlightened, an expert, and one who operates in love, using all the gifts and abilities inside of me. I am working daily toward personal mastery.

You may recall that your mission is, in fact, your purpose. As you move through life with a firm consciousness of your sense of purpose (i.e., your ability to create the type of life you envision for yourself), you are developing mastery of your best expression of you.

The values you identified in the last chapter continue to be your guideposts toward the greatest expression of you. As you consciously choose to live out your values and be true to your values, you will live in alignment with principles that will keep you grounded as you carry out your vision and mission.

> YOU BECOME YOUR MOST DOMINATE IMAGE IN YOUR MIND. YOU BECOME WHAT YOU THINK ABOUT THE MOST.
>
> *- Lou Tice*

I realize that I keep using the word "conscious." It is because, unless you are self-aware of the foundational elements of your highest self, you may find that you are covering a lot of territory but are really not going anywhere. You may aimlessly go in this direction and then in that direction without a clear sense of what you are trying to accomplish.

Funnel your energies into your personal mastery for developing the ultimate expression of you. Energy ignites passion that serves as fuel to accomplish great things.

We usually don't spend time in the normal course of our daily lives developing personal mastery. However, I invite you to master the definition of the greatest expression of you–the image and the associated emotions–through daily repetition, until you eventually become your greatness.

You can handwrite your definition or print it out, then run your fingers across the words on the paper. The key is to be mindful when you rehearse your greatness. It will probably feel a little weird. It may feel phony. Just notice what you are experiencing and keep going with it. Eventually you will mirror your definition as your internalize and embrace it as truth.

The good thing about your mind–your subconscious mind–is that it doesn't know the difference between reality and what you're imagining. You can imagine and create the life you want, and as you stay with the awareness of who you are becoming, your subconscious will accept this new state as truth. There is no distinction. [2]

But you have to do your part and believe in you, keep it in your awareness, and take actions congruent with your definition of your greatest self. If you rarely explicitly think about your greatness, your mind will gravitate to what is experienced in your day-to-day life.

As you develop personal mastery of the highest version of you, you may find that you increase your self-acceptance, self-awareness, and self-responsibility. As you own all dimensions of you and accept all outcomes, you become the chief architect and designer of your destiny.

MASTERY LEADS TO CONFIDENCE

Confidence does not come from a feeling of confidence. Confidence results from action, mastery of a certain skill or image.[3] We're talking about mastering "You."

Confidence also comes from making decisions that lead to the accomplishment of your vision. You now have a clear sense of purpose and direction, a straightforward path to achieve what is most meaningful in your life. Confidence is the result of taking inspired action toward your purpose and mastering the greatest expression of you.

> MY PRESENCE SPEAKS VOLUMES BEFORE I SAY A WORD.
>
> *- Mos Def*

How would you like to be confident, truly confident without having to "make" yourself feel confident? You have to be willing to put in the work to master yourself–your vision of your greatness–until it becomes so real there is no distinction between what you believe about your greatness and how it shows up on the outside.

Live your vision and mission as if you are experiencing it right now, in the present. The more you can take action toward something personally meaningful to you and something you love, the more you will embody a presence of confidence. However, there are no shortcuts to this process; it takes work, daily reiterating you.

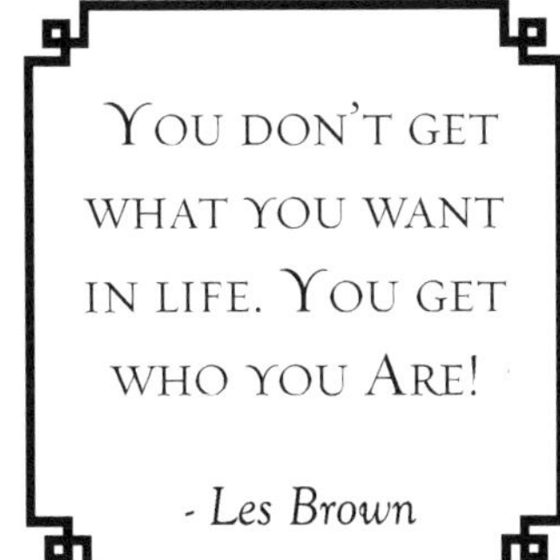

Don't focus on developing confidence. Instead watch how you envelop confidence by taking inspired action toward the greatest expression of you and carrying out your mission. Sear your greatness into every cell of your body. Feel it fully in order to fulfill your

> BE WHO YOU ARE AND SAY WHAT YOU FEEL, BECAUSE THOSE WHO MIND DON'T MATTER AND THOSE WHO MATTER DON'T MIND.
>
> - *Dr. Seuss*

mission. You're starting to feel more confident already.

YOUR POWER PRESENCE

According to dictionary.com, **presence** *"is the ability to project a sense of ease, poise, or self-assurance, especially the quality of manner of a person's bearing before an audience."*

Power presence comes from a confident, self-assured place of knowing who you are and knowing your greatness. It is often a commanding aura sensed in how you walk, talk, and exude confidence in the company of others. Power presence is most evident in individuals who practice personal mastery and have done the inner work that we have been doing throughout this book. The inner work of examining the parts of you that are beyond your title and position in life uncover the highest, greatest expression of you. You effortlessly exude what you have mastered–you–versus allowing others to define you.

When you develop your power presence, you are seldom affected by the "outer" or attached to the opinions and perceptions of others. I am not saying you are not in tune with or aware of the outside, but you no longer are being swayed to and fro by the fleeting estimations of those around you. Your power comes from within and is seared into the very fabric of who you show up as.

Presence is also about being present. Being present means being mindful, alert, clear, intentional about who you are and what you are doing. "The key to peak performance is total engagement in the task."[4] Think about the number of times you were doing something but not fully engaged or speaking with someone and you were "distracted." You will invariably increase your presence when you are present with who you may be speaking with and what you may be doing.

Be conscious and present. Did you know that we are to honor all people, love the brotherhood, fear God, honor the king? (1 Peter 2:17, NASB). Engage with everyone as if he was a king and she was a queen.

There is a third element of presence that gives you your power, but not as man defines power. There is only One Presence and One Power and that is the Lord, God Almighty. When you are one with God, the One Presence and the One Power, you inherit this Power. You have the assurance of God's power, just like you have His unfailing love. All that God is, is available to you. Knowing this truth arms you internally with a self-assurance that you are not operating from your own strength but through the power and strength of God Himself.

Now combine all three aspects of presence:

1) How you project a sense of self-assurance
2) Being present - alert and mindful
3) Being one with God and being cognizant of the Power of God within you

Now you have power presence. Your ability to exude a power presence rests in the extent you are conscious of the three elements of presence. Take them as your own, and walk in this power presence. God predestined you (Romans 8:30) and set you apart for a great work. You have the assurance from God Almighty who knows every aspect of you (Luke 12:7) and the plans He has for you:

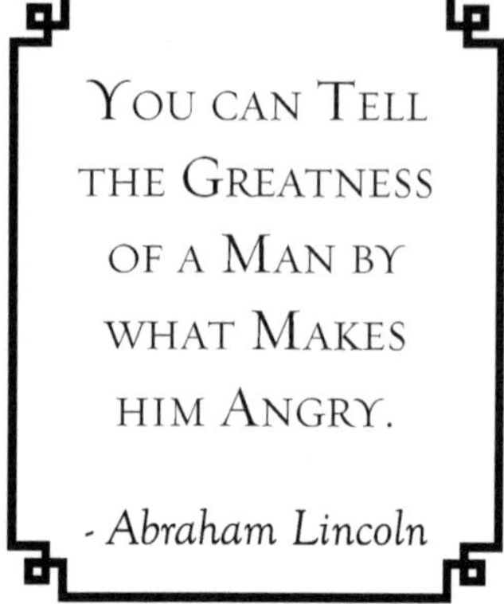

Before I formed you in the womb, I knew you. Before you were born, I set you apart. I appointed you as a prophet to the nations. -Jeremiah 1:5 NIV

For I know the plans I have for you, declares the Lord. Plans to prosper you and not to harm you, plans to give you a hope and a future.

- Jeremiah 29:11 NIV

You are set apart, now own it.

Don't confuse the word power with evil or high and mighty. Power is owning what you know to be true about you, free from others' expectations, wishes and desires for you, good or bad. In owning your own power, you have the right and freedom to design your life the way you see it and want it (your vision).

It is especially liberating not to be confined any longer to another person's often limiting belief about you and their adverse reactions to your uncommon path. Some of the worst offenses are the boxes and perceptions others place you in because of your race, gender, or sexual orientation. Let them be them and you be you. You have this right. Now is the time to own and master you.

YOUR POWER VOICE

Your power voice comes from a place of knowing–knowing who you are, and what your purpose is and speaking from this place. You can then exercise your power voice when you have conviction about what is true or not true for you. You decide what you want and what you don't want and you give a voice to your preferences.

Let your words communicate your truth. Say what you mean and mean what you say. This is your power voice. You then become aligned with your thoughts, words, and actions.[5]

You take actions that are in alignment with what you know to be true about you. And you stop taking actions that are not in alignment with who you are and the greatest expression of you. This is why it is so critical to take the time to develop your script (i.e., the greatest expression of you) and replay it over and over until you become that self.

It boils down to your boundaries. At the core of your essence is your truth and the truth of your being. You have to have measures in place to protect and guard against intruders of your true essence. This includes your own critical thoughts that stir up confusion and doubt in your mind about your greatness.

We sometimes think less of ourselves than we should. Be sold out and committed to owning and becoming closer and closer in alignment to your creative self of the greatest expression of you. As a result, you become proactive instead of re-active. You pre-meditate your thoughts, feelings and actions (based on the highest expression of the greatest you) instead of having your buttons pushed and being reactionary. It's harder for someone to "push your buttons" when you know who you are and where you're going. In fact, no one can push your buttons unless the material on the inside was already primed to be pushed. If someone does "get to you," it will show you where there is more inner work to master. It has little to do with anything or anyone outside of you.

GIVING OUR POWER AWAY

You give away your personal power when you allow another person to impose their standards, their definition or preconceived notion of you, onto you. You give away your power when you don't say what you want to say or express how you really feel. You give away your power when your words don't match up to your corresponding actions. Allow others their freedom of thought, but don't let others impose their thoughts on you.

Here are two examples I witnessed of a young woman and a young man giving away their power because they allowed "society" or "others" to impose their perceptions on them.

The young woman was angry because she felt she had to always defend her "blackness." So she continues to use her power to fight and defend instead of creating and allowing herself to be who she is. She is giving away her power.

The young man, who is also African American and is large in size, personally told me that he has to work to appear less intimidating, taking on a softer tone of voice and body stance, so others won't be afraid of him.

I was saddened because both individuals are giving their power away to people who are operating out of their own fear, which has nothing to do with these individuals.

Do you ever notice how Oprah Winfrey owns her own power? She doesn't apologize for being who she is. Yes, I will admit, Oprah Winfrey is at the top of her game, but she does represent a real role model for what is possible and what owning your power can look like. It will look and feel different for each of you because it is "your" power.

When you own your power, you will have freed-up energy to walk with confidence and stay focused on your mission. You won't be using your power defending or fighting. And you won't be giving away your power either and being silenced.

Trust your inner self–the small voice within, sometimes referred to as your gut or intuition. This response is very close to your true self because it doesn't take into account the external chatter and criticism that is based on outside conditions and others' expectations.

You will need to take time to listen to the small voice within, cultivate a relationship with it through a practice of silencing the outside–the "noise" going on all around you and even in your own mind. A good way to do this is through the practice of meditation. I have provided some resources in the back of the book on the practice of meditation.

Single sisters: Have you ever given up your power to a guy out of a fear of being alone or of a need to be held? Well, I certainly have. You will recall from my story that I gave up my power more often than I needed to because I didn't have a clear sense that I had any power. I didn't operate from my base of power. And I didn't use my power voice to say what I wanted or what I didn't want. Even if I verbally expressed what I didn't want, my actions were not in alignment with my words, so I really didn't operate in my power.

Another way we give up our power is by needing and seeking the approval of others. Elari Onawa notes that we give up our power when we become dependent on an external condition to feel a certain way (e.g., safe, happy, and fulfilled).[6]

For example, young girls, especially those entering middle school and the critical years that follow, often seek the attention of the male counterpart. Sometimes it takes the form of dressing a certain way to get a boy's attention. It also takes the form of girls "dumbing down" (i.e., pretending not to have the right answer or being quiet in class so they will not appear to be smarter than the boys) to be accepted.

Adults play these games, too. For example, do you dress for yourself or do you dress to get the attention of others? Do you join certain organizations for the status it brings more than for the true cause it represents? What about your choice of the zip code you live in or the type of car you drive? These questions are not meant to be judgmental but a check-in to see where you may be giving your power away through your dependency on external objects, opinions, and conditions.

While the ways we give away our power are too numerous to list in this chapter, there is one final way we give up our power as it relates to our greatness: We give up our power when we devote our lives to the things we don't want (e.g., unfulfilling job) instead of focusing our energies on what we really want for ourselves—that greatest expression of you.

Steve Paulina strongly advises you to decide what you want and then focus your thoughts, feelings, and actions on those desires. He challenges: "What false prerequisites have you put in place to block you? (e.g., getting to the right weight, making enough money, etc., before you decide to go after what you really want)."[7] Another author says it this way, "Take mindful action on your valued direction or purpose."[8]

You are more powerful than you realize. Own your power and go after what truly matters to you.

EXERCISE YOUR POWER PRESENCE AND VOICE AND ASK FOR WHAT YOU WANT

I wrote this chapter in a public computer lab. While I was writing, two individuals came in and started talking in loud voices. They may have been unaware that others were working. After hesitating momentarily, I simply got up and politely asked that they keep their voices down. I hesitated because I didn't want a potential confrontation and I was in a public space. But their loud voices were interfering with my work. They apologized and were quiet from that point on.

You may not always get what you want, but owning your power means owning your power. You have to assert yourself, speak up and ask for what you want. No one else in the computer lab made the request. I did. It was a small victory, but guess what? The more you practice owning your power and using your power voice, the easier it becomes. It is just like flexing your muscles; the more you use them, the stronger they become. Repetition, repetition, repetition. Conversely, every time you shrink back, avoid a difficult conversation or request; the easier it becomes to not say anything the next time, too, until you have weakened your voice.

As you get comfortable exerting your power, presence and voice, you will feel more confident when you pursue your mission and ask investors to invest in your business or ask supporters to be a part of your mission. Henry David Thoreau said, "Go confidently in the direction of your dreams! Live the life you've imagined." And I would add two more words: and boldly. Go confidently and boldly in the direction of YOUR dreams!

AFFIRMATION

I stand in my power presence by being conscious of the greatest expression of me. I exude confidence by taking inspired action to fulfill my mission.

TIPS AND STRATEGIES TO DEVELOP YOUR POWER, PRESENCE AND VOICE

- Take time to define and write out the greatest expression of you. Be bold and don't conform to anyone else's standards or expectations.

- Read aloud your definition every morning and every night.

- Develop personal mastery for the greatest expression of you by focusing on your vision, mission and values.

- Take inspired action that leads to the accomplishment of your mission.

- Let the inner work you have done toward personal mastery speak for you as you walk into a room. Walk in your power presence.

- Use your power voice to speak up and ask for what you want. Say no firmly to the things that are not for your highest good. Say yes with conviction for the things you want.

- Own your power. Stand in your power presence and don't give your power away to anyone.

You are stronger, smarter, and more resilient than you think. You are capable of achieving far more than you believe. ***You were meant for greatness*** *— like all of those who have achieved it. But it takes persistence. It takes determination. It takes facing your fears and doing that which is hard and necessary, instead of what is quick and easy. It takes skipping the mythical shortcuts and using your imagination as a map and preview of life's coming attractions.*

- Zero Dean

CHAPTER EIGHT

MENTOR FOR SUCCESS

I am not a teacher, but an awakener.
- Robert Frost

Now that you've taken the time to clearly define your vision, mission and values and you are integrating those elements into every aspect of your life, you may find that you could use some guidance to make the progress you desire. And the right mentor will be able to give you the guidance and encouragement you need.

When I was in high school, I became aware that there were successful, powerful women around me. These women "didn't play." They were on top of their game, they were professional, and they held me to high standards just by their exemplary walk. I discovered I had a natural inclination to be around them. Here's why: When you are attracted to someone or admire someone or admire a quality in another person, it is because you identify with something in them that is already inside of you, just to a different degree. In them you get a preview of the developing you. Most mentors were mentored and are able to see your value and are happy to show you the way.

YOU ARE YOUR BEST MENTOR

But before we talk about being mentored for success, there is something I want to call to your attention. You are, in fact, your best mentor. Here's why: No one knows you inside and out (other than God Almighty) better than you. There are things that you know about yourself that no one else does. There are certain personal things that you are probably not going to disclose to your mentor.

For example, I know for me to be my absolute best, I have to finally conquer my road rage. All of my accomplishments, family, and future potential can be tarnished and wiped out if I am not able to overcome my road rage. This fact would probably never come up in a mentoring relationship. It's a little too personal.

Can you see what I mean? In order for us to get to our ultimate best, which by the way can never really be achieved because we're limitless, you have to leverage the fact that you will always be your best mentor, especially in handling personal issues.

Skills and knowledge can always be obtained and taught, but no one knows your personal business more intimately than you. You will have to be committed to a never-ending journey to personal development that will get you closer and closer to your highest good, to getting real with the core issues that only you and God know will take you to your best.

Take some time right now to journal about this. Come clean and be honest with yourself. Dig deep, but be kind to yourself in this exploratory process.

Here are a few questions to get you started:

1. What do you want to disclose that only you and maybe a small number of people know about you?

2. How is this issue/situation holding you back from being the best expression of you?

3. When you overcome it, how will it catapult you into the next level of your greatness?

4. Who are you being that is not leading you to your desired result of fulfilling your vision for your life?

Thank you for being honest. Continue to work on this area and, as you continue to grow and develop, come back to this simple exercise to keep moving toward your highest level of greatness.

WHAT IS MENTORING?

> FOR EVERY ONE OF US THAT SUCCEEDS, IT'S BECAUSE THERE'S SOMEBODY THERE TO SHOW YOU THE WAY OUT.
>
> - *Oprah Winfrey*

Mentoring is based on a relationship between two or more individuals. A mentor is someone who has walked certain aspects of your walk and can show you the "how to's" reinforced with confident empowerment.

A mentor can be a man or woman, younger or older, and of a different race and other factors than you. Mentoring essentially is helping maximize another human's potential. A mentor helps you stay focused on the endgame of achieving your vision.

"Mentoring is about facilitating change and growth."[1] Specifically, you will benefit from mentoring when you face new challenges and are ready for new growth opportunities. The key here is to grow your vision and find a mentor who can help you see what you often cannot see in yourself. Mentors often "hold space" for you by believing in you and working with you while you learn to masterfully "take up your own space" confidently.

All successful people have mentors. Here are some examples of individuals with mentors who were/are extremely successful:

Plato, Aristotle, Nelson Mandela, Warren Buffett, Bill Gates, Oprah Winfrey, and Steve Jobs.

All great leaders need a mentor. And on the Resources page, I share an article that tells you how to find the right mentor for you.

There are different types of mentors. Most people think of mentors in a corporate setting, like finding a mentor to help you climb the corporate ladder. However, the type of mentoring I'm referring to is to help you execute your vision. If you seek out mentors who help you achieve someone else's vision–like in the corporate world–why not seek out mentors who can help advance your own vision?

> I'VE BEEN BLESSED TO FIND PEOPLE WHO ARE SMARTER THAN I AM, AND THEY HELP ME TO EXECUTE THE VISION I HAVE.
>
> - *Russell Simmons*

Yes, you can use some of the skills and knowledge from a mentor in one setting in a totally different area of your life, but why not cut to the chase? Seek out and develop mentoring relationships with individuals who can help you carry out your vision.

MULTIPLE MENTORS

Did you know that you can have more than one mentor? As a speaker and business owner, I might seek out a successful business owner to help me navigate the world of business ownership as well as a professional speaker to help me learn the nuances of speaking. The important idea here is to go after whatever you need to execute your vision, and realize it may not be found in just one person.

Here's a radical idea for some: How about forming a dream team committed to your vision and growth? How much synergy would be in one place if you brought together different types of top-level advisors? This is how you elevate your game to a higher level and get strategic about your vision.

One of my close friends called a dream team dinner together for me. I serve on this close friend's advisory board for her vision organization, so when she saw that I was going through a "rough patch," she initiated my dream team.

She brought together some very powerful, intelligent women who were already a part of my inner circle. Those women, with their love and compassion and experience far beyond mine, were able to help me see the "me" in the challenge I was facing and to deal with the issue from a different perspective. That, in a nut shell, is what mentors do: they show you "you" in the context of what you are facing by listening and being a sounding board so you can hear "you." They help you navigate rough waters, offering a soft shoulder during difficult times. You get the picture.

Choose three to five top level, trusted, advisor-type individuals and call a dream team dinner or breakfast. Be open and honest with where you are and what you think you need to get to the next level. This is a concrete, strategic step that will help you get closer to your vision.

ADVANTAGES OF MENTORSHIP

We talked earlier about how you are your best mentor, but now let's talk specifically about how other mentors can add to your life and help you fulfill your mission.

Mentors can share their experience and journey, helping you navigate ill-defined paths to success, and providing emotional support as you stretch yourself to fulfill your mission. Effective mentors will also share their mistakes and mishaps to shorten your learning curve.

Mentors often have well-established and diverse networks that they may be willing to share with you. Often they will open up their Rolodex and connect you with their contacts who can lend expertise or be of service to you in other meaningful ways.

Mentors give you a broader perspective, helping you see new opportunities and providing you with encouragement and know-how to execute your expanded vision.

HOW TO ESTABLISH A MENTOR RELATIONSHIP

The fundamental aspect of mentoring is a relationship. Relationships are key to business and life success. Therefore, it is important that you seek someone who is grounded, has wisdom, and has demonstrated a measure of success throughout his or her journey.

> RELATIONSHIPS REQUIRE CULTIVATION AND CULTIVATION REQUIRES TIME.
>
> *- Audrey J. Murrel*

"Relationships require cultivation and cultivation requires time."[2] You can't establish a mentor relationship on the "first date." You have to get to know someone for who they are, and not because you need someone to show you the way. Does that make sense?

Think about successful people in your life and seek to make a genuine heart connection with them. You might start with a chat over tea. Ask them about themselves, what they value, how they got started, and who their mentors are. Ask about what challenges they faced along their journey and how they overcame obstacles.

As you get to know them, then you can share more about you, your vision, and what you think you need to get closer to executing your vision. Then you can ask them to be your mentor.

It is important that you have clear expectations about what you want from the relationship and, equally important, what you can give to the relationship. Some examples of having clear expectations could include the frequency of meetings, maintaining confidentiality, responsibilities of and determining the progress of mentees.

Here are some examples of what mentees can do to give back to their mentor: you can send an article or blog post related to their vision or career, or make a personal introduction to someone in your circle of influence who can advance their mission. If you can't think of anything, you can always offer that you are open and ready for success and will implement their advice (provided it is sound).

Be sure to keep a mentoring notebook to capture their advice in a central place. This small act alone shows that you value their input. And it helps you to be able to refer back to it and not have to hunt all over for your notes. You need to always show your appreciation and gratitude for their mentorship.

Sometimes a mentor will seek you out. Here is a practical way that I approached someone I wanted to get to know and how she was seeking me out simultaneously.

I attended a women's leadership workshop. There was a panel of leaders sharing their stories, with some sharing more intimately than others. I emailed all of the speakers to comment on their talk and request a coffee/tea chat. One of the speakers, who I had introduced myself to at the end of the workshop, agreed to have tea with me. It turns out that her mentor, who knew me well, had "assigned" her to mentor me. That was amazing.

This mentor is sharp, professional, and full of insightful advice. She helped me through a difficult period of time in a work-related situation, for which I am especially grateful.

It's one thing to get a mentor to help you advance in a career or position in order to fulfill someone else's vision. It's quite another experience to receive mentoring to execute your own vision! Make sure you are putting your energy in the right arena.

YOUR ROLE IN A MENTOR RELATIONSHIP

Your role is to prepare and do your homework before you meet with your mentor.

If this is a new mentoring relationship, be sure to send over a résumé or one-sheet summary of "who you are," your vision, and potential areas where you may need some assistance and guidance. Note: this type of preparation does not negate the importance of and time needed to get to know a prospective mentor as highlighted in the preceding section.

Don't miss the opportunity to research your mentor. Find out on your own their "story," background and accomplishments. Then you can have a meaningful conversation and start to build a solid relationship.

Never get too comfortable with a mentoring relationship. Always come to your meetings, phone conversations, or Skype with an intention. It is not the mentor's role to take the reins of your interaction.

How impressive would it be for you to email your mentor your introductory documents as mentioned above and provide an agenda for your time together? Now you are speaking your mentor's language. Their time is extremely important and often limited. Therefore, you will set yourself apart and generate more support because of your efficiency and the recognition and respect you show for your mentor's valuable time.

Be open and honest about where you are and what you need. This is not the setting to put on an impressive face. You are seeking mentorship to get to a higher place, so there's no room for pretense in your interactions with your mentor. Trust your mentor to recognize that you have not quite arrived, which is why you are seeking their input and guidance. It is okay not to have it all together. Be open, honest, and "real." It will save you and your mentor a lot of time and you won't have to backtrack over areas that you glossed over trying to impress them early on.

Implement what you mentor recommends for you to do. This is the highest compliment you can give them! Also, if something is not going as the two of you have talked about, then reach out to them to "course correct." You don't have to wait for another formal interaction. Keep the momentum going. And only request a new meeting after you have completed the prior assignment or implemented the previous advice.

Be sure to show your mentor what you have accomplished, not just when you meet, but also between formal meetings, which can be done via email. This serves as a measure of accountability for you.

Express your gratitude for the advice and time often–both in small ways (thank you notes) and more demonstrative ways (such as buying breakfast or dinner) or in some way that you know matters to them. For example, maybe you have learned that your mentor is an avid reader (which most mentors are), then what about a gift card to a bookstore?

Remember that mentoring is all about relationship. Nurture your mentoring relationship frequently (once a quarter at a minimum) with updates and coffee/tea chats, for example.

Whatever vision and mission you are working on, there is someone who is capable of helping you accomplish it. Be open to asking for help and assistance. Accept the fact that you don't have to have all of the answers to get started. This fact stops so many people from moving ahead in pursuing their mission. Remember, you are the visionary, but there will be others who can show you the way–like how to build a team of supporters, how to raise funds, and how to manage your time, etc.

Mentoring for success is part of the journey. As you move closer to your mission, you may find the need to let some mentors go and seek out new ones. This process often happens naturally. Always be open to growth and change. Your mentor will not be offended when the time comes for you to seek out new mentors for continued growth. You're well on your way to higher heights and deeper depths by being mentored for success.

One parting comment. As you are being mentored, remember that one day it will be your turn to mentor someone, to advance and support their vision. The law of reciprocity states that whatever kindness has been extended to you, you will need to extend to another. Keep this in mind, because as you grow into your greatness, you will attract others who will see you as the experienced mission-driven leader. Expect it.

AFFIRMATION

I attract the right mentor at the right time to help me advance my vision and I am grateful.

TIPS AND STRATEGIES FOR YOUR MENTORING RELATIONSHIPS

- Recognize and accept the necessity to be mentored to success in order to reach your highest potential and to advance your vision.

- Remember that you are your own best mentor. Spend some time journaling the important aspects of you that need to change in order to go to the next level of success. Be honest and kind.

- Seek out individuals who are successful in advancing their own vision. Spend time developing and nurturing a genuine relationship and then ask to be mentored.

- Honor and respect your mentor's time. Take written notes in a central place when you interact with your mentor and properly thank your mentor regularly.

- Don't pretend that you have it all together when interacting with your mentor. Ask for help to advance your mission. Leave the "got it all-together" face at home.
- Form a dream team of 3-5 top level, trusted, advisor-type individuals to develop higher-level strategic planning for your vision and personal success.
- Recognize the lifespan of mentoring. As you grow and your vision grows, you will need to seek out new mentors. Your mentor's job is to help you get to the next highest level. He or she will be okay if you have to "fire" them.
- Be open and ready to become the Mentor when it's your turn, sharing from a genuine and generous place to help others grow and develop into their greatness and advance their mission.

Mentorship is the key
to extraordinary success.

- Mike Murdock

CHAPTER NINE

UNVEIL YOUR BRILLIANCE

There's nothing enlightened about shrinking so that other people won't feel insecure around you. - Marianne Williamson

IMPORTANCE OF OPERATING FROM BRILLIANCE

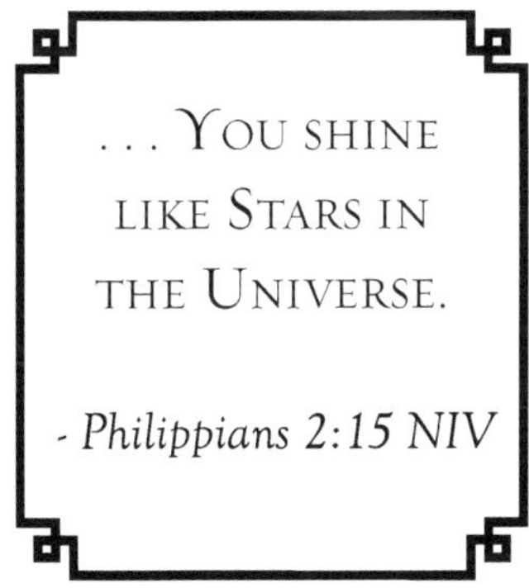

You're doing great!

Before you move forward in expressing more of your greatness and executing your vision, I have to alert you that, as you do, you will shine brighter than you ever have before. The more clarity you have surrounding your mission and vision, the more your brilliance will shine through—just like a diamond with a flawless clarity rating.

Your shining brightly will transform lives, create and innovate, and solve some of the world's problems. People who really need, and can benefit from, your vision can find you. Collaborators and investors can find you more easily as you shine more brightly.

Therefore, as Marianne Williamson implies in the above quote: Who are you not to shine, to shrink back?

WHY YOUR BRILLIANCE THREATENS

You have been through life's challenges and are emerging into the fullness of your true purpose.

> PEOPLE MAY HATE YOU FOR BEING DIFFERENT AND NOT LIVING BY SOCIETY'S STANDARDS, BUT DEEP DOWN, THEY WISH THEY HAD THE COURAGE TO DO THE SAME.
>
> - *Kevin Hart*

Remember that as you step into and express your brilliance, some people will see you as a beacon of light, helping them see their way to a new life. Yet others, the unawakened, will view your brilliance as a threat to them, because they don't have what you have on the inside.

The unawakened are those who don't know how to or decide not to move past what's holding them back; individuals who are not yet committed to pursuing a meaningful, purpose-driven life and unveiling their own brilliance.

In order for your brilliance not to overshadow, outdo, or outshine these individuals, they may attack you. No, not physically. But with sharp words that may sting. Or possibly by withholding information, sabotaging, discriminating, turning their back on you, alienating you–any ploy that will allow them to retain their sense of self and well-being.

People engaged in these ploys subconsciously base their sense of self–and their judgment of you–on their hidden beliefs about success, gender roles, race, failure, etc. Whether their attacks are intentional or subconsciously influenced, let's call these individuals "brilliance blockers."[1]

I have personally been in environments where just my presence was viewed as threatening–not because of anything I was saying or doing that was actually threatening anyone. But when you have a clear sense of who you are and you are not obligated to the "powers that be," then you carry yourself differently, you perform above the status quo, you are outspoken and some people will resent you for all of that. And to make matters worse, we women also bring with us our beauty, grace, and intellect.

> SOMETIMES YOUR LIGHT SHINES SO BRIGHT THAT IT BLINDS PEOPLE FROM SEEING WHO YOU REALLY ARE.
>
> - *Shannon L. Alder*

If you are in an environment that cannot contain your greatness, there are a few likely scenarios that may result:

You may lessen your brilliance in order to fit in and make those around you comfortable.

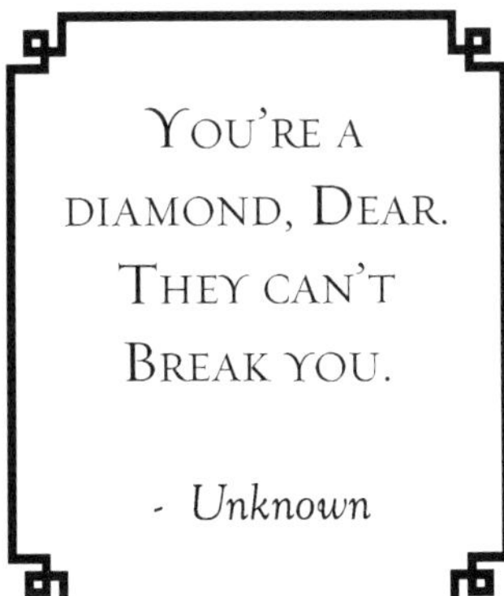

You may continue to be your bright self until someone in authority knocks you down to size so you fit in with everyone else around you.

You will run. You will either find another container you fit into or, hopefully with the material you are being exposed to in this book, you will never again allow yourself to be boxed in where those who are still veiling their brilliance will be comfortable around you.

I personally witnessed a strong, beautiful, black woman forced to "shrink" by the system she placed herself in. Those around her told her she talked too loud, she was too direct, they told her when to stand up and when to sit down, and to overall "tone it down." It was truly sad to see it all play out. Fortunately, this strong, black woman ran and did not stay where she could not shine–like many of us are doing or have done. She regained her strength and devoted more of her energy to her "true" purpose, which has evolved to a new, higher level in God.

You have to get to a place where you are able to spot another's insecurities, resistance, closed-mindedness, authority attachment, undeveloped level of consciousness and not allow it to "knock you off your square." You have to see through people and see where they are and recognize that their number one job is self-preservation–to ward off all threats to their sense of self.

Also know that every situation and perceived challenge with another person is essentially all about you. It is a reflection shining back on areas where you need to grow. It's not about the other person. The challenge shows you areas you need to cultivate. It also shows you where your compassion falls short.

As we grow in brilliance, our capacity for empathy for others should naturally increase. You become more at ease with your brilliance and more sensitive as to when and how you need to encourage the brilliance in others. Therefore, your threat level lessens.

There have been two times that someone verbally attacked me. The first time was before I was awakened and I fought back verbally, each of us escalating in intensity and volume. The second time someone attacked me verbally, I was in my awakened self, and could see instantly that I had unintentionally insulted the person and I immediately apologized.

My apology was accepted, but I was also given a stern lecture for my waywardness. Fortunately, I could also see this person's deep insecurities and chose not to engage.

Since I could see where the person was, I certainly was not going to energetically engage this person in their survival-based emotions (i.e., fear, judgment, competition, etc.). I did my part, which was to rectify the situation and take ownership for my perceived mistake. I then felt compassion for the person, silently, because I knew they had not yet started to unveil their brilliance.

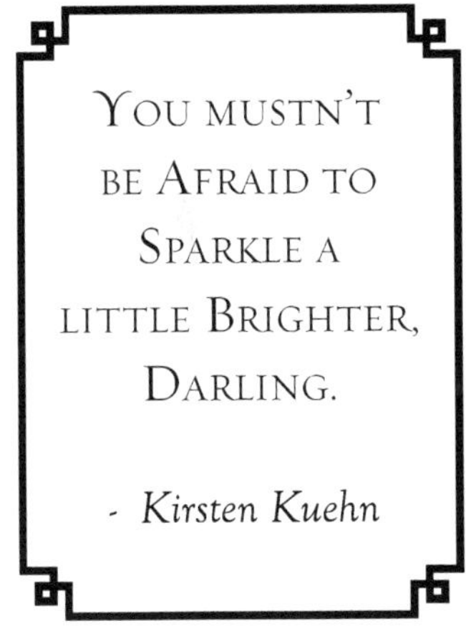

When you know your purpose and are committed to fulfilling it, you will not have time or energy to invest in others' ways of being. Know that these people have not yet "awakened." Never allow yourself to be energetically entangled with people who are not for your highest good.

WAYS TO OPERATE IN YOUR BRILLIANCE

Here's the challenge: surround yourself with people who are "bigger" than you: people who walk with ease in their greatness, and who are not shy about letting their brilliance shine brightly. I know this can take you out of your comfort zone. But these giants also know how to make others feel good about themselves (e.g., Oprah Winfrey) and they also know when to leave people in their mediocrity or unawakened life.

Also know that if your light is the brightest in the room, you're in the wrong room. Keep elevating yourself into spaces where other bright lights shine freely and comfortably. Don't get comfortable and confident being the brightest light in the room. You need to continue to feel a slight bit of unease as you approach new and unfamiliar situations and people.

I once had dinner with a former school superintendent. She is a "giant" of a person and I really didn't know how the dinner was going to "flow." Surprisingly it flowed just fine because I have greatness inside of me and so does she. She could easily see that I was bringing something to the table just by the fact that I approached her and invited her to dinner. Don't shrink back at another's greatness. Step up to it.

Being a giant can be a lonely path–so can being a pastor. Surprisingly some pastors are actually lonely because they are often surrounded by lots of people jockeying for position, who profess their love for them. But very few of these people feel worthy enough to get to know the "true" pastor, so the relationship remains superficial.

Some people assume that pastors already have close friends and thus the majority of people don't personally reach out to them in any meaningful way. If you think everyone is inviting the pastor over to their house for Thanksgiving dinner, think again.

My pastor's wife and I had dinner once. It was lovely. At one point during the evening, she reached out and put her hand on top of mine and confessed she didn't have very many friends and extended an invitation for us to be friends.

At the time I was in my unawakened state, not fully knowing my greatness. So I immediately rejected her offer and politely corrected her, "Of course you have friends." She replied, "No, I don't." She went on to explain that those "friends" that hang around her are not "true" friends. They really don't know her at an intimate level.

Well, that was all fine and dandy, but surely she couldn't think that I could be her friend. I was a "girl" in my mind and she was a beautiful, established woman pastor with "big" pastor girlfriends. Who in the world was I that she had the audacity to insinuate that we could actually be friends? Even girlfriends? How preposterous.

And yet how sad? I hastily dismissed her because I couldn't fathom that she needed to establish a heart connection with me. She clearly saw something in me that caused her to want to establish a deeper connection. You never know where people are. She risked and I rejected.

Once you recognize and accept your brilliance, you'll be conscious of it and not allow it to trip you up or trip others up. You have been endowed with greatness for a reason. Don't miss an opportunity to change lives or add to lives because you haven't become empowered to operate in your greatness.

Don't take yourself too seriously as you move forward in your brilliance. Here's a personal example that shows that eventually we appear "brilliant," even when we mess up, because our brilliance is who we really are.

A prominent karate school Grand Master requested that I provide a speech at a black belt promotion ceremony. In the speech I was to share my experience about being a mom of a soon-to-be awarded 1st degree black belt son. I was all ready to go on stage but I was also listening out for calls from my invited guests who had not arrived and possibly needed assistance with parking and finding the right location in the building. I "talked" my last guest into the building and put my phone into a slot in my portfolio case, the same portfolio case that contained a copy of my speech.

Well, I was well into my speech on stage when low and behold my phone rang. It was my Mom asking about my son's performance. Can you imagine? Here I was in my professional element, trying to be funny and engaging and my phone rings.

I instantly thought of the Grand Master and thought, oh gee, he is probably thinking this is totally unacceptable. I quickly rebounded with a joke and kept going as if it never happened. Later that afternoon at a post-event party, people were complimenting me on the speech and some said, "When the phone rang you seemed real."

Again, you are bound to stand out when you are operating in your brilliance, whether you intend to or not, but never get too far ahead of yourself because we are all prone to mistakes, no matter what level we achieve.

Giving thanks for your greatness and the great things that you are accomplishing every day is another way to operate in your brilliance. If you are in a state of greatness, then you send signals to the universe that the events have already come to pass. As you give thanks in advance of these things, you "emotionally condition your body to believe what is producing your gratitude has already happened"[2]

Surround yourself with other giants so you start to feel at ease with your greatness and you will share and leverage it to brighten up dark places and reach people that others cannot. Let your brilliance burn brightly.

Notice people and situations when/where your brilliance threatens and become aware of situations/people whose brilliance threatens you and causes you trepidation. Have compassion for developing souls and move closer to people that cause you hesitancy–because that, my friend, is where your next growth edge lies. Accept your greatness. Unveil your brilliance. Embrace it, nurture it, and expand it.

AFFIRMATION

I shine bright like the stars in the universe with ease to serve others and make a difference.

TIPS AND STRATEGIES TO UNVEIL YOUR BRILLIANCE

- Be conscious of your brilliance and let it shine brightly.
- Don't shrink back from your greatness. Keep elevating it.
- Be aware of how your brilliance threatens certain people in certain situations. Take care to help others unveil their brilliance.
- Surround yourself with other "giants" of greatness for support and learn how to walk in your greatness with ease.
- Don't be the brightest light in the room. Find new spaces to grow your brilliance.
- Don't allow your greatness to trip you up or trip others up. Accept it and treat it with care.
- Give thanks ahead of events as if they have already happened successfully. This is what it means to operate in a state of greatness.

Once you accept, embrace
and completely own the incredible
being you were born to be,
you will discover in the depths
of your soul the power you've had
all along to express and claim your
own unique brand of brilliance.

-Sherri Bishop

CHAPTER TEN

DISCOVER NEW TRAILS FOR GROWTH

You will either step forward into growth, or you will step backward into safety. - Brian Tracy

GO TO THE NEXT LEVEL

You have started along a journey to come back to yourself and have made tremendous progress. However, once you get to a new level, there is always another level waiting for you. There will always be another level to attain or one more lesson to learn. Why? Because your growth potential is limitless.

There will always be more of you to express. There is an endless amount of love inside of you to express to others who need love, there is more grace for you to obtain, greater health for you to experience, more wisdom to acquire, more acceptance to embrace, more humility for you to walk in.

You are becoming everything you believe yourself to be. And it has no end. As you get comfortable with or master one

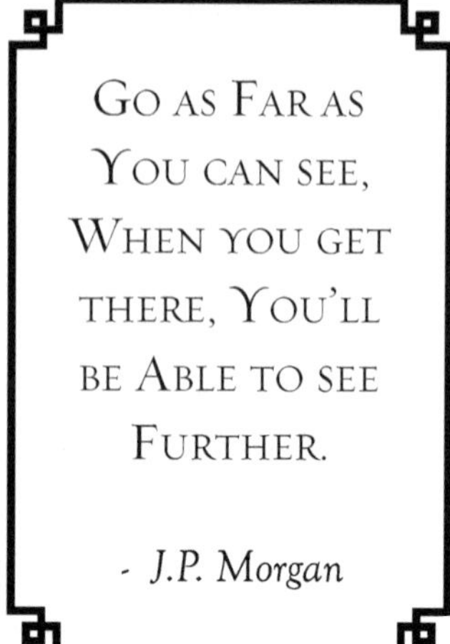

level of a chosen task or passion, there is always something new to explore, always something to challenge your limits. Growth is ever expanding and changing.

It is important to keep in mind, as you travel along your journey to becoming yourself, that you and God are one. Therefore, as you thrive in God, you will come to know that your growth is limitless, as God is eternal - no end. As you reach a certain destination, once you get there, you'll be in a new higher place and able to see even more. There is no end point in your journey to self-actualization–becoming all of what you believe yourself to be.

Your growth in God and your potential are unending and ever expanding and ever evolving. There are no limits in God, The Infinite One; therefore, there is no stopping the growth process. But without challenge, there can be no growth.

But grow in the grace and knowledge of our Lord and Savior Jesus Christ. -2 Peter 3:18, NASB

When you think of challenge, do you think of easy, comfortable, a walk in the park? Or do you think of demanding and out of my comfort zone?

When I went away to graduate school, it was not overly difficult, but it was a challenge. And oh, did I grow.

In graduate school was when I first learned of my racial and gender identity, if you can believe it.

A challenge presses against the status quo and generally accepted notions. A challenge typically involves a change in our emotional state, in our circumstances, and it requires exertion of physical and/or mental effort.

The good news is that with a balanced amount of challenge and support you will achieve optimal growth in your endeavors.[1] Your job is to keep growing. So embrace your challenges.

Take a few minutes now to write down areas in your life where you could use some additional growth. Challenge yourself. Go deeper and higher than you have gone before. Consider these questions during your reflection time:

1. What would be a stretch for me to achieve in the next three years?

2. How do I use my bulldog determination in the face of a challenge I'm experiencing?

3. What beliefs do I have that are holding me back from going to my next growth level?

4. What ineffective habits do I need to break and what habits do I need to develop for maximum growth? (e.g., time management, organization, procrastination, follow-up, etc.)

5. What circles of influence do I need to grow into?

6. Is it time to find a new mentor to help me grow at a higher level? If so, where will I look?

7. What books do I need to read to expand my knowledge base or elevate my mindset?

8. How can I spend more time in meditation or quieting my mind for higher and deeper revelation?

Have you ever accomplished something big like earning a degree, or winning a difficult case, or closing a big deal? The natural tendency is to take a big exhale and coast for a while, until the next big task comes along. Sometimes it's called "resting on one's laurels."

Well, we are going to take a different approach. We are going to map out your milestones for growth so that you will know what is next on the agenda. We'll also talk about taking time to celebrate and renew a little later in this and subsequent chapters.

Count it a tremendous blessing that you have been chosen to still be alive, to be given a new day. This fact alone should indicate your enormous potential for greatness and continued growth.

Imagine waking up each morning fully appreciating the work ahead of you, the privilege, the joy in knowing you are connected to an infinite God who knows your path.

For I am confident of this very thing, that He who began a good work in you will perfect it until the day of Christ Jesus.
- Philippians 1:6, NASB

Before I formed thee in the belly I knew thee; and before thou camest forth out of the womb I sanctified [set apart] thee, and I ordained [appointed] thee a prophet unto the nations.
- Jeremiah 1:5, KJV

God has set you apart and appointed you to fulfill a great purpose. Your continued growth will be a tremendous blessing to those in need of your achievements. You may not fully realize it but you are the answer to someone's prayer. What an incredible privilege it is to answer the call and change someone's life through your continued growth journey.

> SOMETIMES IN LIFE, YOUR SITUATION WILL KEEP REPEATING ITSELF UNTIL YOU LEARN YOUR LESSON.
>
> - *Brigitte Nicole*

YOUR GROWTH IS IN THE LESSON

I received my first lesson in the workplace from a wise and seasoned supervisor. During my annual performance evaluation, my supervisor gave me the highest rating because my work was excellent. I was happy. Then as the "formal" part of the performance evaluation ended, she said: "Chanel, you're like an ostrich with its head stuck in the sand. Come out of your office and let people get to know you and you get to know other people."

The people around me were there to help me accomplish great things, but I never took the time to really get to know them. The people closest to you (i.e., your team members) will have your back when needed, if you have a relationship with them.

It was a valuable lesson, but one that I did not appreciate at the time because I was just too focused on the work. So guess what? I was presented with another opportunity to learn this lesson.

If you fail to learn a lesson, rest assured. You will be granted another opportunity.

Since I didn't learn it the first time, I had to repeat the same lesson. Only this time, instead of someone gently whispering in my ear like the supervisor I referenced above, I was "sat down" (a phrase taken from the Baptist church—it's what happens when you are in a high position and get out of line) and then I really got the opportunity to know my team.

This time my role and duties were cut by 80%, including all of my appointments to committee work inside and outside my office. I was now a "resident" (in the office) team player and I had no choice but to get to know my team, up close and personal.

Let's face it, losing 80% of your role leaves sufficient time to chat it up with your co-workers on a daily basis. Once I accepted the change, I authentically let myself be known and took the time to nurture relationships with my team members. In everything give thanks; for this is God's will for you in Christ Jesus (1 Thessalonians 5:18, NASB). Amen.

Here's the point. Your new trails for growth will not diminish if you are seeking greatness. In fact, you will be tested and tried until you come out as pure gold.

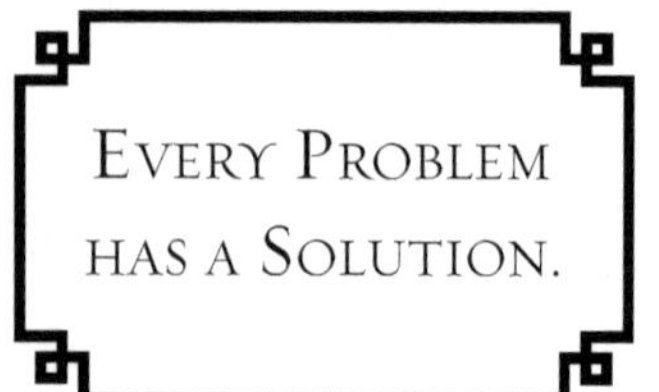

There are no shortcuts to this refinement process. There is no skirting a problem or adjusting down to the level of a problem.

Additionally, whatever you resist persists and whatever you embrace changes. If you fail to heed the lesson the first time, chances are the stakes are only going to get higher until you grow bigger than the problem or challenge you are facing.

GROW BIGGER THAN YOUR PROBLEMS AND CHALLENGES

Ralph Waldo Emerson is quoted as saying, *"Don't be pushed by your problems. Be led by your dreams."* Growing bigger than your challenges requires that you don't focus on your problems.

Whatever you focus on expands. So rather than focusing on the problem, focus on the solution. However, don't approach the challenge with the same mindset that created the challenge. Seek out a bolder, more expansive mindset to think of options to grow beyond the challenge.

Focus on taking massive action in the direction of your dreams, your mission. Remember that challenges come to spur us on to greatness. Don't lament or give your energy to problems. This misplaced energy only fuels the problem to grow bigger, which is what you don't want to happen.

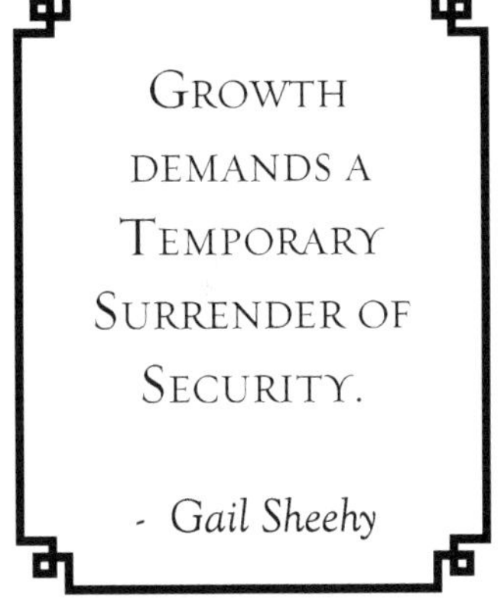

Focus on what you want and spend the time in prayer, seek wise counsel, and take massive action to move beyond the challenge to the solution. As T. Harv Eker says, *"The size of the problem is never the problem. It's always the size of you!"*[2] T. Harv Eker is the author of the bestselling book, **"Secrets of the Millionaire Mind,"** motivational speaker and businessman. His teachings have helped over 1.5 million people move closer to obtaining financial freedom.

The opening quote for this chapter: "You'll either step forward in growth, or step back into safety" is worth mentioning again. My older brother, Rev. Louis Crowder, delivered a message in his home church on a return visit during Thanksgiving 2015. He admonished the congregants not to stay in ankle deep water where it's safe and requires no commitment and no dependency on God. Rather, he challenged them to venture out to deep waters, where you have to put in more effort because you have to swim, use your faith–and where you may feel less powerful.

The question in this context is are you going to go back to the shallow waters or grow in the deep waters? In other words, are you going to stay on the cliff or are you going to jump and grow wings on the way down?

If you're going to rise to the next level, you will need to take risks and leave the familiarity of certainty. At the new level, you will not have all of the answers. You may not know all of the nuances but, *"Never let the fear of striking out keep you from playing the game." -Babe Ruth*

At the writing of this chapter, I just ended my last day at my full-time job–a position I stayed in for over two and a half years because I was chained to a paycheck. Meanwhile, I knew I could be more and do more. Finally, I took the leap of faith and submitted my resignation so I can pursue my speaking, writing, and coaching business fulltime.

As I was passively bemoaning to a friend because I was still cleaning out my office at 9:51 p.m. on my last day, my good friend replied, *"Enjoy turning those lights out! When you turn those off, others will turn on."*

> REMEMBER TO CELEBRATE THE MILESTONES AS YOU PREPARE FOR THE ROAD AHEAD.
>
> *- Nelson Mandela*

This statement was profound and it gave me the needed energy and motivation to wrap things up and "turn off the lights." The very next morning, I felt an increased sense of freedom and expectancy for even greater things to come. I took a risk and I believe it's going to pay off in a major way as I impact and influence lives.

MARK AND CELEBRATE YOUR ACCOMPLISHMENTS

It is very important to mark and celebrate when you attain each new level, goal, or mission. When your objective is to achieve a new growth level or new goals or a new mission, plan ahead and decide how you are going to celebrate its completion. Review your future celebration daily with vivid imagery.

Create a vision board that not only portrays the actual vision you have for the future but also includes ways that you will celebrate its completion. In your meditation time, imagine how you will feel celebrating your great accomplishments. Let this imaging touch every cell and organ in your body with feeling and enthusiasm, every morning and every night.

Remember this from Oprah Winfrey, *"The more you praise and celebrate your life, the more there is in life to celebrate."* Don't gloss over your accomplishments. Record them.

Keep an "accomplishment journal," recording the event as well as how you felt upon its accomplishment. Then, before you start along your path of continued growth, pursuing a growth area you identified in the beginning of this chapter, go back and reread your journal. You can use the same emotions from a previous accomplishment to thrust you toward the new, unfamiliar goal. It is a process called, "flip up, flip back."[3]

Your aim is to get better and better, stronger and stronger, and wiser and wiser. Step up to your challenges with the power already on the inside of you and with your vision ahead of you. You will be unstoppable and have tremendous impact.

The more impact you amass, the faster you will amass more people to impact. Therefore, you will need to regularly engage in new and higher level growth activities that spur you along to make an even bigger difference in the world.

AFFIRMATION

I step forward in growth daily and I feel accomplished and fulfilled.

TIPS AND STRATEGIES TO DISCOVER NEW TRAILS FOR GROWTH

- Accept the fact that your growth is unending and plan for it.
- Spend time reflecting on your accomplishments and digging deeper to uncover new areas for growth.
- Start an "accomplishment journal" and record and review your achievements daily.
- Don't "coast" after you achieve something great, waiting around for the next milestone. Chart the next growth milestone and go after it.
- Learn "the lesson" thoroughly so you won't have to face it again.
- Grow bigger than your problems. Take massive action toward and stay focused on your dreams.
- Remember: Every problem has a solution.

- Use the "flip back, flip up" strategy to project the same emotions from a previous accomplishment into a new and unfamiliar goal or setting.
- Take time to celebrate after a major accomplishment.

And the day came when the risk to remain tight in a bud was more painful than the risk it took to blossom.

-Anaïs Nin

CHAPTER ELEVEN

MAINTAIN HEALTH AND WELLNESS

Beloved, I pray that in every way you may succeed and prosper and be in good health [physically], just as [I know] your soul prospers [spiritually]. – 3 John 2 (AMP)

> A WISE MAN OUGHT TO REALIZE THAT HEALTH IS HIS MOST VALUABLE POSSESSION.
>
> - *Hippocrates*

You're doing great. You've been working from the inside out. Now we want to express on the outside how great you're feeling on the inside.

The health of your body is extremely important. In fact, I believe it is second only to the health of your soul and spirit.

There are no shortcuts to achieving and maintaining good health. There is no magic pill. The way we look and feel is a result of the lifestyle choices we make on a daily basis.[1]

Your physical body is a part of your wholeness, your 'presence.' It is not an area to be neglected.

Read again the scripture quoted above. Why would the writer of the book of John admonish its readers to be in good health? I believe it's because good health is foundational to a life of vibrancy and purpose.

CONNECTION TO YOUR BRILLIANCE

Your true brilliance and greatness are inextricably connected to your health. When you are not worried about or having to "look" after your health with doctor appointments and medication because of pain and suffering, you can use that energy to accomplish your goals and purpose. It is freed-up energy you can apply to your greatness and to generate creativity.

There are individuals who are in reasonably good health but burn the candle on both ends. They are a part of the over-achievers club. They often work long days and well into the night, eating on the run and getting little exercise, cutting back on sleep to accomplish goals, responding to emails at 2:00 a.m. Over time, the habits of this lifestyle can lead to disease.

Barbara Jean, a wise cousin of mine, once told me that while I can burn the candle on both ends in the short-term, it will come with a cost to my long-term health. You are infringing on your future health and longevity when you adopt a fast-paced, always on the go, stressful lifestyle. And an article about personal mastery on HubPages states, "Failing to deal with stress during its starting stage can eventually lead to chronic stress."[2]

Joe Dispenza (we heard from him back in Chapter 3) shares here about the potential long-term effects of an unhealthy, stressful lifestyle: "If you're putting the bulk of your energy toward some issue in your external environment, there will be little left for your body's internal environment. Your immune system, which monitors your inner world, can't keep up with the lack of energy for growth and repair. Therefore, you get sick, whether it be from a cold, cancer, or rheumatoid arthritis. (All are immune-mediated conditions.)"[3]

I know you want to live life to the fullest, and being healthy allows you the mobility and stamina to create a successful life. And being healthy and fit will add to your longevity, allowing you to live out your purpose longer–potentially seven years longer. As noted on the American Heart Association's website: "People who are physically active and at a healthy weight live about seven years longer than those who are not active and are obese."[4]

There is an old video of Bobby Brown, former member of the popular boys' band, *New Edition*, when he was in shape and able to out-dance practically anyone. But recently a video of him went viral when he couldn't keep up with his former band members during a reunion tour. He was completely out of shape and not able to fulfill his mission–performing.

Can you see how being in shape can affect your purpose?

BEING HEALTHY AND FIT IS ALL ABOUT YOU

Being healthy is first of all personal. Don't allow anyone to put demands on your body. I admonish you to make you the priority, not the desires of others, including your spouse.

There are women who go to great lengths to lose weight for their husbands. Some that I know personally have gone on diets because their spouse "laid down the law." He determined she was carrying too much body fat after pregnancy or no longer fit the model he was attracted to over 20 years ago. In my opinion, a husband needs to accept his wife as she is and then encourage her through his love and support as she progresses on her quest to be healthy and fit.

Once you're in shape, your body speaks for itself. Until then, don't go on fad diets to fit into a dress for a reunion or alter your body because of others' expectations of beauty. You define you. No one else does.

> EXERCISE IS KING. NUTRITION IS QUEEN. PUT THEM TOGETHER AND YOU'VE GOT A KINGDOM.
>
> - *Jack LaLanne*

What does it mean to be healthy? Being healthy is simply being fit and taking care of you. It's not a matter of weight, specifically. It's about aligning your physical being to your inner being.

I will say it again. It's not a weight issue. Please don't confuse the concepts.

On its website, the World Health Organization defines health as "a state of complete physical, mental and social well-being and not merely the absence of disease or infirmity." The word **health** comes from the word **hale**, which means *wholeness and strong and healthy*.

Health is also made up of your overall lifestyle, how you take care of yourself. A good example would be regular exercise, good nutrition, adequate sleep, as well as an absence of smoking and consuming excessive alcohol and/or drugs.

Have you ever gone to your high school reunion? What did you observe? I'm sure many of the alumni had gained weight and perhaps looked older than their age.

Have you ever seen a man or a woman who drinks excessively or smokes? Do they look like the picture of health?

I've already mentioned the effects an unhealthy lifestyle had on Bobby Brown. But what about the tragic life-ending effect it had on Whitney Houston and Elvis Pressley? A healthy lifestyle is critical to continuing your life.

That is why I include this chapter on health and wellbeing in this book. Because it is vitally important that you maintain your health and wellbeing in order to live your life fully and to accomplish your purpose and mission.

Do you get regular medical check-ups? Visit the dentist every six months? Get regular breast exams? What about working out or exercising at least three to five times per week? Examples of exercise could include dancing, walking, running, and swimming. The key is to be active.

What about your nutritional intake? I love food just like anyone else, but I certainly know when I am indulging in foods that are not healthy for me.

It's important to become conscious of your eating habits. Do you eat to feel good? Do you eat more when you are depressed or sad or anxious? The first step to break food addictions, like any other addiction, is to become aware of the triggers that prompt the unhealthy eating.

For example, around 3:00 p.m. every day during the workweek, I used to go to the vending machine and buy a candy bar–a habit that cost me five dollars a week. It was certainly a habit and I was fully aware of it. After almost 2 ½ years of this unhealthy, feel-good habit that I used to get me through the afternoon, I was able to "kick the habit."

It started on my 50th birthday, when I gave up my 1-2 a week Boston cream donut habit. I took my children to the bakery to start my birthday morning and I walked out of the bakery without purchasing one donut for me.

Then at a women's conference in California a few months later, after eating a few pumpkin spiced, cream cheese filled muffins, I had had enough. I declared from that moment on that I wanted to be conscious and feel whatever pain I was "sugar-coating" with feel-good sweets. Instead, I wanted to feel the discomfort so I could do something about it.

Forty-five days later I resigned from my full-time day job. To keep myself conscious of my knee-jerk reactionary response to grab something "sugar-coated," I vowed not to eat another chocolate bar or sweet pastry–including Mom's sweet potato pies and rum cake–until I break the million-dollar mark.

I suggest you decide to implement one healthy habit at a time. Introduce a colorful blend of more fruits and vegetables into your diet. Get help from a nutritionist, use online web resources, or talk to healthy friends. Being healthy always seems like a point of discussion.

Being in shape affects how you carry and present yourself. It determines what jobs you will go after and your confidence in approaching people.

I do not recommend going on a diet to lose weight. Instead I suggest trying to maintain the freed-up version of you and then develop a reasonable plan to achieve optimal health. The definition of optimal health might include a discussion with your healthcare provider.

> EVERY TIME YOU EAT OR DRINK, YOU ARE EITHER FEEDING DISEASE OR FIGHTING IT.
>
> - *Heather Morgan, MS, NLC.*

I know there are determinants of health that include a person's level of education, socio-economic background, and environmental conditions. I will not address these factors here because I want you to focus on behaviors within your control. There are a lot of them. I want you to be the best you and then you can expand your influence and make changes in the other factors.

What are the behaviors under your control? What do you need to change in your health regimen? Do you have a health regimen? Have you thought of hiring a personal trainer or joining an exercise group so you'll feel supported as you get started?

Develop a consciousness for health and your behaviors will start to line up with your consciousness. When we don't have a regimen for health, we don't do healthy behaviors like exercise. When we don't have a consciousness for eating well, we'll eat the donuts and the birthday cake at the office gatherings. But we can take simple steps to make small changes when we make up our minds that we are going to live true to our inner being–which is now freed-up.

Have you ever known someone who worked so hard that he/she neglected their health? Working long hours, eating out and on the run, and getting little sleep? Sure, at times we all have big projects that require us to put in extra hours at work and maybe eat fast food. But if this is now your lifestyle, your health will eventually absorb the effects. Many young women and men have died prematurely because of disease associated with a stressful lifestyle. Don't become one of them.

YOU INFLUENCE YOUR HOUSEHOLD

It is important to set a good example for your family and children to follow. In general, women are primarily responsible for feeding their children. Babies develop eating habits primarily from their mothers. Even in the womb, a developing fetus starts to acquire a taste from the mother's diet through the amniotic fluids the fetus ingests.

There is a rather common notion that if we want our children to eat their fruits and vegetables, then we must first make these choices ourselves and provide a positive, stable eating routine. If we buy cookies and eat more than the child does, then we have to examine our behaviors and our triggers for eating.

Our little ones are watching our behaviors and attitudes regarding food very closely. For example, before I went cold-turkey to give up my sugar addiction with sweets, chocolates, and pastries, I would eat more Elmer Fudge Striped cookies than my kids. I would sternly let them know they could only have three at the very most. Hypocritically, I would grab a whole section and take them to work and eat all of the cookies in one sitting. Both children would "call me out" on my hypocritical eating behavior.

When you have clarity about the importance of choosing and eating healthy foods like fresh fruits and vegetables, whole grains, proteins, fish and lean meats, and de-emphasizing processed lunch meats and boxed foods, sugary snacks and juices, then you are having a greater impact on your child's growing body and brain development. You are also shaping habits for the teenage years, when you are not always around, and even into their adult life when they will have to make independent choices.

I have learned, though, not to be too restrictive–like withholding dessert unless my kids ate something green on their plate. This restrictive behavior can cause a dislike of the very food item you would like them to eat.

The bottom line is to make healthy food choices, eat healthy routinely in a positive environment, and have kids help with meal planning and preparation to increase their buy-in.

LOSING WEIGHT

If you ask one hundred women if they currently desire to lose weight, what you do think would be the response? I believe 98 out of 100 women would reply that they want to lose weight. Instead of focusing on the weight for now, let's take a look at another indicator of overall health: body mass index or BMI.

BMI is a calculation using your height and weight that provides you with a rating of your overall health. While there is some debate over the accuracy of this measurement, it is generally believed to be a good indicator of your risk for diseases such as heart disease, stroke, type 2 diabetes, osteoarthritis, and some forms of cancer.[5]

The CDC provides the following ranges for BMI values for adults:[6]

BMI	WEIGHT STATUS
Below 18.5	Underweight
18.5–24.9	Normal or Healthy Weight
25.0–29.9	Overweight
30.0 and Above	Obese

You can get a rough estimate of your BMI by entering your weight and height into the WebMD's BMI calculator. I have included the web address for this tool on the Resources page in the back of this book.

You can also take a measurement of your waistline. "According to the National Institutes of Health, a bigger waist circumference (greater than 40 inches for men and 35 inches for women) is linked to a higher risk of type 2 diabetes, high blood pressure, abnormal cholesterol levels, and heart disease when BMI is 25 to 34.9."[7]

Have you noticed that your body composition has shifted, with more fat landing and staying in your mid-section and hip areas? The portion of muscle decreases and the portion of fat increases as we age.[8]

This shift causes your metabolism to slow down, and for some people with less physical activity, it is easy to see why we gain weight in all the wrong places. You don't want your weight to slow you down and keep you from going after opportunities because your confidence is shaken.

Just as we mentioned earlier when we were talking about being in shape, your weight can also affect your confidence, because how you "present" to the world is often based on how you feel about your body.

It is a commonly held notion that most psychologists and counselors agree that body image affects your self-esteem. When you feel strong and vibrant, you carry yourself differently (i.e., you have a healthy self-esteem). You are more willing to participate in physical activities, you are not so restrictive in your selection of clothes and you more readily go after opportunities and jobs because you feel confident in your appearance. And your body image certainly can impact your readiness to date or meet new people.

The more positive you feel about your body and your weight, the more comfortable you feel in your skin and the more willing you are to express all of you.

If you don't make your health a priority, you will continue to forfeit more and more of your time and energy dealing with health challenges.

There are many articles and books that can give you more research and facts about BMI, weight, and fat. The important take-away is that until you have a personal, meaningful reason to be healthy and fit, chances are you'll get on or continue to stay on a dietary treadmill, without the real lasting lifestyle change you desire.

Please take a few minutes to ask yourself the following questions, being honest and "real" about your health. You can use these questions as conversation starters with a health care professional.

- Why do I want to be healthy?
- If I desire to lose weight, why?
- When was my last physical examination?
- When was my last dental check-up?
- When was my last breast exam?
- How many times a week do I work out?
- Do I put my exercise routine on hold when I have other pressing priorities?
- Do I have an exercise buddy?

BARRIERS TO MAINTAINING HEALTH AND WELLNESS

Let's start by calling a spade a spade. We come up with a lot of excuses for not making our health a priority. But at the same time, we make time for and pay for the things we value.

Let's look at a few of the many barriers to maintaining health and wellness and some ways to overcome them.

Time

A major barrier to regular fitness and exercise is a lack of time. You may have child responsibilities in the morning and then you may be too exhausted in the evening to exercise. I know, we have all been there. But remember, every problem has a solution. Get creative.

Before I had child drop-off duty in the morning, I attended a 6:00 a.m. yoga class three times a week. Can you get up earlier to exercise? If you don't have a partner to alternate workout time with, enlist the help of another mom and exchange exercise favors with each other. She watches your kids while you work out and then you do the same for her. If this does not work, you can take both families on a walk through a park or around the block a couple of times. The important thing is to get moving.

Motivation

Instead of thinking about or having to "workout," start doing an activity that you actually enjoy: bowling, swimming, golfing, bike riding, dancing, walking, etc. Build this activity into a regular routine of moderate intensity, five times a week for 30 minutes each time.[9]

Self-consciousness about Your Body

Take a buddy with you when you workout for empowerment. You can exercise at home with a video for a while before going to the "gym," for example. As you get more active, you will increase your confidence. As you see results, you'll want more of the "active stuff" and you will become less self-conscious about how you look.

My Hair

India Arie, American Soul and R&B singer, has a popular song entitled, *"I Am Not My Hair."* She says that instead she is "a soul that lives within." We let the aftermath of our hair affect our decision to exercise or not.

Do you know how many girls and women, particularly African Americans, have never learned how to swim because of their hair? Don't let your hair interfere with your physical activity. Find ways to manage your hairstyle or workout on the days between your hair appointments. There are no excuses because of your hair.

What are your barriers? There are many others like laziness, boredom, money, etc. Whatever your barriers are, ask for support to develop a way around them.

You do not have because you do not ask God.
-James 4:2, NIV

Remember, your health and wellness are vitally important.

LOVE YOURSELF TO HEALTH

Love is pure energy. Show lovingkindness to yourself and your whole body. As you love yourself and your body, you will naturally do and give energy to things that manifest that love and concern.

It is very important that you understand that love transforms, completely, even your body.

My sister, please don't neglect your health. Your presence is important. Your mission is critical to the world. Put in the time and do the inner and outer work to get healthy and maintain a healthy lifestyle so you can fulfill your purpose.

> Show Lovingkindness to Yourself and your Whole body. As you Love yourself and your Body, you will Naturally do things that Manifest that love and Concern.

AFFIRMATION

I love everything about me, including my body. I make time to take care of my body through proper eating, rest, and exercise. I feel incredible.

TIPS TO BECOMING HEALTHIER

Here are ten ways you can make immediate changes in your health. These changes take into account that you have already been doing the inner work described in the preceding chapters.

1. **Make a health and wellness plan.** Determine the reason(s) you want a healthy lifestyle and internalize it every morning, every night, and multiple times during the day.

2. **Be physically active.** (Walk to your car, take the stairs, swim, dance, mow the grass, walk in the park, play with your grandchildren, get moving.) Thanks to Newton's first law of motion, we know that a body in motion tends to stay in motion. Dan Buettner, a National Geographic Explorer, who studies centenarians (people who live to be over 100 years of age), found that centenarians move their bodies a lot![10] Simple.

3. **Be conscious and make healthy food choices at every meal and every snack**. Bring an alternative healthy food choice to the office birthday party, have an apple, drink water, have a salad with your meal (you'll get full faster), give up one unhealthy item at a time (e.g., remember my Boston cream donuts?).

4. Avoid overeating. Dan Buettner also encourages us to stop eating when our stomach reaches 80 percent full in order to avoid weight gain.

I know it feels good to keep eating when the food is so tasty and delicious. But when you're almost full, get up and walk away; don't keep sitting and eating until you are about to bust. When we do this over and over again, we accumulate fat.

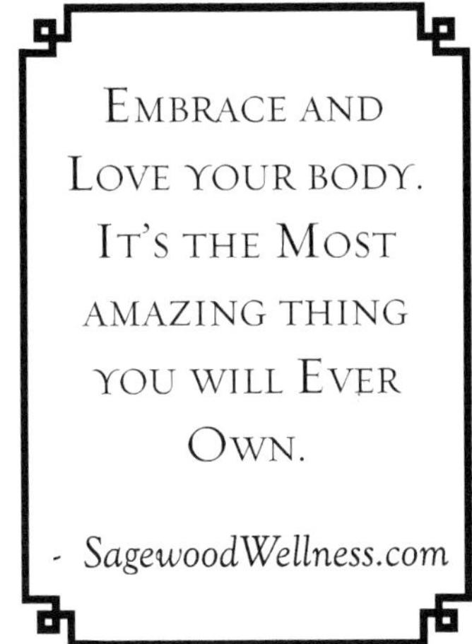

5. Take time to de-stress. Take a brisk walk, meditate, go on a gratitude walk, exercise, sleep, do nothing.

6. Schedule and attend your annual physical examination. Talk to your doctor about getting healthy.

7. Hire a personal trainer and/or a nutritionist to help you develop a workout and nutrition plan and provide support and accountability as you achieve a healthy lifestyle. You can also find many online resources in these areas.

8. Love and accept your body in its current state. Your body is a part of the whole you. Love all of you. Don't compartmentalize pieces of your body. Eliminate any negative words about your body.

9. Keep a health and wellness journal to record your health plans and goals, progress, and feelings you experience related to maintaining your health and wellness.

10. Reward yourself (at the spa) when you accomplish a health and fitness goal.

Warning: Exercise has been known to cause health and happiness.

- Popular Gym Poster

SECTION 3

PURSUE A LIFE OF PURPOSE

CHAPTER TWELVE

PRACTICE HIS PRESENCE

In the early morning, while it was still dark, Jesus got up, left the house, and went away to a secluded place, and was praying there. -Mark 1:35 NASB

Wow! Look how far you have come. You are learning to recognize and honor your feelings, you are healing, and you are operating in your mission and your purpose in freedom and continued growth.

Take a deep breath.

Now imagine exhaling in the presence of God or into the arms of God, letting go of all of your cares and strife. Do you feel a sense of calm? A sense of lightness?

As you achieve and accomplish all you were designed to do and become, realize it is all a vehicle for you to get closer and closer to God. The challenges and the triumphs are the backdrop for the true high calling, which is to be in conscious union with God, because in Christ is all of the fullness of Life (Colossians 2:6-8).

Do you realize that each higher level you aspire to requires increased trust in God, a new measure of faith, and often a

willingness to surrender and "let God take the reins?"

Do you also know that great people spend significant time with God? Now is the time to turn the volume down from the external and retreat inwardly. In other words go within (you).

Going within allows you to not have to be in control and it offers you an opportunity to turn the reins over to God. Going within and being in the Presence of God has tremendous benefits: "You make known to me the path of life; in your presence there is fullness of joy; at your right hand are pleasures forevermore (Psalm 16:11, ESV). This promise from God is enough to make me want to continually bask in His Presence... forever.

Going within also gives you the opportunity to "Seek the LORD and his strength; seek his presence [His face] continually!" (Psalm 105:4, ESV). God is omnipresent, which means God is present everywhere at all times (Psalm 33:13-14). Another way I've heard it said is, "There is no spot where God is not."

You have continuous access to God, but the challenge is maintaining your conscious connection to our Ever-Present God. Ultimately, "Our supreme need is to know God."[1]

I believe there are two primary ways to get to know God: through His word and through prayer. There are different ways to use these avenues to get to know God better. Let's explore a few.

I believe there are two primary ways to get to know God: through His word and through prayer. There are different ways to use these avenues to get to know God better. Let's explore a few.

PRACTICING THE PRESENCE OF GOD THROUGH HIS WORD

This Book of the Law shall not depart from your mouth, but you shall meditate on it day and night, so that you may be careful to do according to all that is written in it. For then you will make your way prosperous, and then you will have good success. - Joshua 1:8, NASB

This scripture is very straightforward and is one that many of us are very familiar with. However, do you include time in your daily practice to meditate on God's word? In addition to reading God's word, meditating on it includes quiet contemplation, reflection, and application.

In your quiet time, preferably first thing in the morning before the "noise" starts, read a Bible passage and "put your mind" completely on that particular scripture. In other words, sit with it before moving on to continue reading. Let the words saturate your being. Ask the Holy Spirit for divine revelation of what the scripture is speaking to you. The word of God brings us closer to knowing the true and living God. And the side benefits are nice too: your way will be made prosperous and you will have good success!

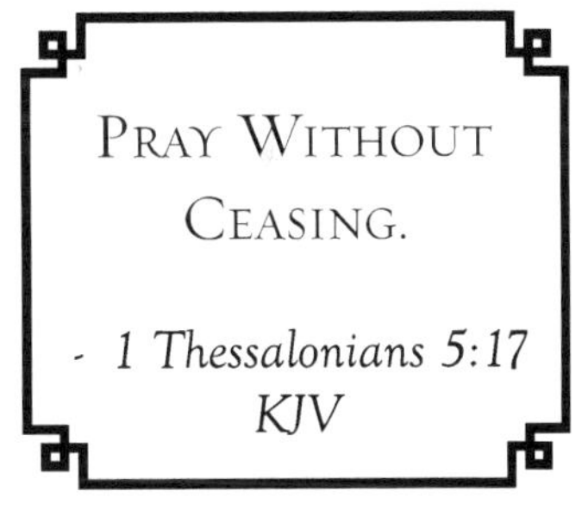

PRACTICING THE PRESENCE OF GOD THROUGH PRAYER

The Bible instructs us to pray without ceasing (1 Thessalonians 5:17), which means to have continuous communication with God.

Many of us think of prayer in so many different ways; for instance, having a certain posture to assume, starting and ending a certain way. But there is no one right way to pray to God.

Your communication with God is yours alone, between you and God. He hears every word you utter and knows every thought you think (Psalm 139:1-5). The important insight to capture here is that as you pray without ceasing, you are in a continuous conversation with God, and therefore, you are being "present" with Him and practicing the Presence of God.

PRACTICING THE PRESENCE OF GOD THROUGH MINDFUL MEDITATION

[BE] "THOUGHT-FULL" OF GOD, WHERE OUR THOUGHTS ARE FULL OF GOD.

- *Fr. John A. Hardon, S.J.*

[Be] "thought-full" of God, where our thoughts are full of God. [2]

Meditation is one of the practices that many of us know is beneficial and wish we would take more time to engage in. However, for some, it has varying connotations, namely associated with New Age and Eastern Religions (e.g., Buddhism), which may be a deterrent to the practice.

I am a strong advocate for the practice of meditation, so much so that I implemented a meditation program at my previous employer where a skilled practitioner led the faculty, staff, and students through mindful meditation during the lunch hour twice a month.

According to Wikipedia, the word **meditation** comes from the Latin word **meditari**, which means "to concentrate." In this chapter, meditation can come to mean to concentrate on scriptures, reflect on the goodness of God, or any other aspect of God–His love,

His word, His grace, etc. Here is a useful scripture to guide your thoughts in meditation:

> *Finally, brethren, whatever is true, whatever is honorable, whatever is right, whatever is pure, whatever is lovely, whatever is of good repute, if there is any excellence and if anything worthy of praise, let your mind dwell on these things. - Philippians 4:8, NASB*

Another form of meditation involves being still and/or silent:

> *Cease striving and know that I am God; I will be exalted among the nations, I will be exalted in the earth. (Psalm 46:10, NASB) or Be still and know that I am God. (ASV)*

You can commune with God in silence. You don't have to do anything but just be and just be alone with God. Some people report, "I don't feel anything." In that case, whatever happens or doesn't happen is just fine. You don't have to expect anything to happen or to feel anything is happening. This is the power of just being.

Learning to just be is new for many high achievers, but that's okay. Try it and practice, practice, and practice some more.

Surrender your thoughts. Settle into the stillness and allow this stillness to expand. This gives you access to your inner knowing. There's such a richness inside of you. You have the Spirit of the Almighty God on the inside of you. As you quiet your mind, you can bring to light what is already inside you. The more we practice meditation, the more audible God's still, small voice will become and the more capable we will be of hearing it.

You may want to try this strategy. Go into your silence, your stillness and breathe in and breathe out, consciously. Watch each inhalation and each exhalation. Notice your thoughts. In the beginning of your practice, your mind will be busy going about its normal activity with a flurry of thoughts. That is what your mind's job is: to think. Initially, you will just observe the thoughts. Thought: "What I am going to cook for dinner?" Another thought comes: "Did I take the meat out of the freezer?"

Then, just like we discussed when talking about your secret pain, imagine you're sitting on the edge of a calm river. As each thought enters your mind, place the thought on a leaf, place it in the water and watch it float away gently until it disappears around the river's bend. Take each thought and place it on a leaf. Detach from each thought and do not judge yourself for having thoughts while you are trying to meditate or become still. Judging will only give you more thoughts to judge.

If you are new to meditation, you will grow in the practice until you can readily still your mind without going through the leaf exercise. When you do and as you do, you will be in a better place to hear from God and be more sensitive to His leading. The only reason we are not always in tune with His leading is because of all of the noise and all of the "externals"– the job, the business, the kids, the traffic, the hustle and bustle, Facebook, you fill in the blank.

What we're striving to do in our time of meditation is to render the external irrelevant. When you practice the presence of God, the external is irrelevant. For that moment in time, go inside and retreat to and take solace in God and His Presence. Don't worry, everything will be waiting for you when you return.

As you evolve in your meditation practice, your life will become a walking meditation with God, where you are in continuous communion with God in everything you do and in all of the thoughts you think.

PRACTICING THE PRESENCE OF GOD THROUGH THANKSGIVING

In every thing give thanks: for this is the will of God in Christ Jesus concerning you. -1 Thessalonians 5:18, AKJV

The meditation of gratitude is very powerful, because in the moment that you are expressing gratitude or thanksgiving, you are present. Hopefully, you can connect your being "present" with the Giver of all things (James 1:17). Then, in that connection, you are practicing the presence of God. Just think if you were to string hundreds of moments of thanksgiving together? As Zig Ziglar said, "The more you are grateful for what you have the more you will have to be grateful for." And that means you will be in the Presence of God even longer.

> ONE OF THE BEST WAYS TO PRACTICE THE PRESENCE OF THE LORD IS TO THANK HIM ALL THE TIME.
>
> - *Joseph Prince*

Therefore, in all of the good and in all of the challenges, give thanks. And we all have challenges and crosses to bear. My car was totaled on Friday the 13th, in November 2015. When it happened, I was immediately thankful for my health and being able to walk away from the accident. Even though the air bags deployed, they never touched me. I was also thankful that no one involved in the accident was injured and I had already dropped my kids off at school. And in about two weeks, I was very thankful to be driving off the car lot in a new car.

Do not be anxious about anything, but in everything by prayer and supplication with thanksgiving let your requests be made known to God. And the peace of God, which surpasses all understanding, will guard your hearts and your minds in Christ Jesus. - Philippians 4:6-7, ESV

FIND GOD IN EVERYPLACE, IN EVERYTHING, IN EVERYONE.

- *Bo Sánchez*

Take everything to God in prayer and thank God for every situation.

As she wrote about in her online gratitude journal, Oprah Winfrey noted the difficulty of the climb to build a new television network and losing sight of "being grateful for simply having a mountain to climb."

The fact that you have a "climb," or that you have a "thorn in your side," means you are in position for great things to unfold. Everyone is not equipped to stand up to a mountain. Some tremble at it, some veer around it. But if God brought you to it, trust that He will bring you through it, victoriously. His word says,

No temptation has overtaken you that is not common to man. God is faithful, and he will not let you be tempted beyond your ability, but with the temptation he will also provide the way of escape, that you may be able to endure it. -1 Corinthians 10:13, ESV

You are strong enough to respond to each challenge you face. For this reason, be thankful you have a mountain to climb. And in each conscious thought of thanksgiving, be "thought-full" of God. This is our primary task as we grow in the grace and stature of God.

PRACTICING THE PRESENCE OF GOD IN EVERYTHING

For many of us, our lives are an ongoing flurry of activity. In days past (before I came back to myself), I could go practically all day without having a single thought about God, except at my meal and snack times, when I said a prayer of thanksgiving. So setting an appointed time to "stop the flurry," to go and meditate and become still, is a treasure for people like me.

In addition to having an appointed time to meditate, Pastor Rick Warren reminds us that we can practice the presence of God in everything, in every task, in every activity as we are mindful of God in the midst of everything we do.[3] When we brush our teeth, when we take the trash out, when we are putting our kids in a time-out.

In all thy ways acknowledge him,
and he will direct thy paths. - Proverbs 3:6, ASV

When we acknowledge Him in all of our ways, we are practicing the presence of God.

Remember God is always there, and He is everywhere. So in everything, acknowledge Him. It can be so simple. Slow down, be conscious and be consciously connected to Him in everything.

Come close to God, and God will come close to you.
- James 4:8, NLT

Take some time to journal your answer to this question:

How do I anticipate my outer life changing as a result of increasing my conscious connection with God?

IDENTIFY AND ADDRESS BARRIERS TO PRACTICING HIS PRESENCE

While so many of us long for a deeper, more intimate relationship with God, often times the day-to-day cares of this world get in the way. We can go hours focusing on a task and forget to be "present" with God, whose Presence is right there with us. We forget to acknowledge Him in all of our ways. We may hit the floor running in the morning, send up a quick prayer, "run" the entire day, only to utterly collapse at night with a "Now I lay me down to sleep" prayer.

On a deeper level, some of us avoid getting "quiet" before the Lord because there is still some "unfinished inner business," some inner hurts we don't want to surface in the quiet. If we stay busy, distracted by the noise, we can continue to discount and ignore those hurts so we can maintain control and "keep it all together." Others don't know what might surface if we sit still too long. We don't want to be "out-of-control" so we continue our control by not totally surrendering to the unknown.

These are real barriers that are standing in the way of our practicing the Presence of God and going within. God already knows about your barriers, your secret pain, your need to stay in control. Now is a good time to turn all of that over to Him. He is powerful enough, strong enough and compassionate enough to handle it all.

Casting your cares upon him, for he careth for you.
-1 Peter 5:7, KJV

God is also patient and will always be there whenever you are ready to trust Him and surrender everything to Him. Ask Him to help you in this area and seek godly counsel for additional assistance.

It is no accident you are reading this book and this chapter at this time in your life. Believe in Divine timing and know that God desires you to go within and reach Him like never before. Practicing the presence of God through His word, prayer, meditation, with thanksgiving, and in everything you do, will bring you fullness of joy and pleasures forevermore.

AFFIRMATION

I am consciously connected to God in everything that I do. I give thanks in all things and I experience fullness of joy and pleasures forevermore.

TIPS AND STRATEGIES TO INCREASE YOUR CONSCIOUS CONNECTION WITH GOD

- Pray without ceasing. (1 Thessalonians 5:17, KJV)
- Keep a prayer journal. Record your heart-felt prayers, thoughts, pains, and desires. Write down your reflections and re-read them to remind yourself of God's faithfulness.

- Identify and overcome any barriers to practicing the Presence of God. Take those barriers to God and ask Him to help you overcome them. Seek godly counsel as needed.

- With each breath, thank God.

- Give thanks for every situation and be "present" with God when you are giving thanks or expressing gratitude.

- Keep a gratitude journal. Every morning and/or every night, record five things that you are grateful for. Re-read your entries often.

- Tell someone how much you appreciate them. Just say, "I appreciate you."

- Give God the First Fruit of your day: Start the day in prayer, meditation, and thanksgiving. Wow! You won't believe the change this can make.

- Build a meditation room or convert an unused or infrequently used area into a meditation room.

- Create a designated place at work to meditate. (Some employers provide a meditation or a reflection room.)

- Sit before the Lord in stillness and just be.

- Now set your mind and heart to seek the Lord your God. (1 Chronicles 22:19, ESV)

- Sing a song of praise to the Lord.
- Ask God to help you stay consciously connected to Him.

The Success of God's work through you is intimately related to the reality of His Presence with you.

-God-Still-speaks.com

The more conscious of God's presence, the more I feel like being myself, the less conscious of His presence, the more I feel I need to prove myself.

-R. T. Kendall

CHAPTER THIRTEEN

ATTRACT THE LOVE YOU WANT

Let all that you do be done in love.
-1 Corinthians 16:14, ESV

CAUTION

If you are not freed-up, or in the process of becoming freed-up, please do not enter into a new relationship. When you are ready, continually operating from a freed-up level of consciousness, you will attract what you seek. If you connect with someone prematurely, you are short-circuiting the process and will continue to attract at the level of the false-version of you, not the whole, free, and joyous you.

> BECOME THE LOVE YOU WANT SO YOU CAN ATTRACT THE LOVE YOU DESIRE.

You don't want to once again become entangled energetically with someone at your old level, because you will eventually come to yourself and outgrow the person you connected with at the level of the false version of you.

Now you want to present your best self when you decide you are ready for love. Please be patient and become the love you want so you can attract the love you desire.

> So we have come to Know and to believe the Love that God has for us. God is love, and whoever Abides in Love abides in God, and God Abides in Him.
>
> *- 1 John 4:16 ESV*

BE LOVE AND RADIATE LOVE

Let's face it, we all want love. Some of us crave love so badly we would do almost anything to get it and keep it. Fortunately, you are no longer in that place. You have grown and have emerged with a clear sense of who you are and what you want on your terms.

Now let's turn our attention to getting you the love you desire. Actually, it's not that complicated.

At one point in my life, I craved the security of being embraced or held by a man. I wanted to be held constantly and I paid the price for that need of false security. What do I mean? There was a longing inside of me that I thought could only be met by being completely immersed in a guy. This was a lie – a dependency that satisfied my longings for only a short time.

It doesn't take a rocket scientist to know that when a man holds a woman for an extended period of time, there are certain physical reactions that typically occur in him: an erection and a desire to release the built-up pressure through ejaculation. Even though I was clear that I did not always want sex, it is very difficult for most men to withstand this physical closeness without a sexual release.

As I became a freed-up woman, I no longer needed to be held. I found the purest love through the love of Jesus Christ and then through my husband. How? By availing myself of God's presence, which is pure love.

God is love and His love radiates in all directions at all times. His love is always available to you if you open yourself to Him and become consciously aware that He loves you.

Once you become clear about who you are and what you want, love can flow from inside you to the outside. As it does, it attracts and mirrors love back to you. You become like a force field of pure love. Believe me, there are other individuals with force fields on the same level that will pick up your love signal and be attracted to you, because similar energies attract.

> DELIGHT YOURSELF IN THE LORD AND HE WILL GIVE YOU THE DESIRES OF YOUR HEART.
>
> *- Psalm 37:4 ESV*

That's what I meant earlier: it's not that complicated. You will radiate an aura of love 360 degrees in all directions around you. As you become love, you attract love. This is the simplicity of love.

When I think back to how my husband and I met, it was because I radiated love and so did he. Essence to essence, we were attracted to each other. If you remain closed to love, love can't get in. As you grow impatient or disillusioned with the process, you may either continue to close yourself off to love, even subconsciously, or you may make choices in haste or prematurely, and end up with a relationship comparable to a half-baked cake. Don't open the oven before the cake is done.

BE CLEAR ON WHO YOU WANT AND CO-CREATE WITH GOD THE DESIRES OF YOUR HEART

Your job is to stop aligning your energy with love interests at a lower frequency than yours. Be open to and, if necessary, seek out those energies that are similar to or higher than yours.

Here is an example: When I hit the dance floor, I immediately start scoping out the good dancers. I can spot them immediately. They are spinning themselves or spinning their partner frequently and in multiple spins or there is a lot of interlocking of arms. In addition, there is an air of confidence, of "owning" the dance. This is attractive.

Those are the only people I approach to dance with me. Why would I ask someone who is not on my level? I always seek out dancers who end up being instructors, because I am "attracted" to their vibrational energy. I want to dance with someone who has a higher skill level than me.

When it comes to love, there is a certain level of physical attractiveness that hopefully abounds. I am certainly attracted to my spouse Gary, but it wasn't his looks that captivated me–and he is physically attractive. I became attracted to his aura and love energy, his caring and his compassion.

We cannot always "see" love. However, when it abounds, then yes, I believe you can see it through the "eyes of love." For example, I knew that I had finally found the real deal when I could literally see the love of God in Gary's heart. There was no doubt in my mind that this was it for me. We have now been married 18 years and I'll be married to him until death do us part.

Don't skimp here. I literally wrote out a list, as advised by a good male friend, of everything I wanted in a guy. I didn't hold back and I didn't rationalize my standards. Remember to always be true to yourself–the real you. For example, if you don't want a guy with kids, write it down. If you want a guy who is "saved," (i.e., someone who has accepted the Lord, Jesus Christ, as Lord and Savior. See John 3:16). Write it down. (See resource section if you desire to be "saved.")

I trusted my friend and literally did exactly what he told me to do. I wish I had kept the list. I vaguely remember putting down that I didn't want a guy with kids, didn't want a smoker and wanted someone who was saved. And I'm sure I put down that I wanted a guy who could love from the depths of his soul.

All I know was, as if by magic, and almost immediately, "the guy" showed up. Here is the insight that my friend shared with me: Once you make the list, you have to determine your top must haves and the things you absolutely do not want. The top four things that I wanted were absolute. There was no compromise. For example, I would not settle for a guy who didn't have children but smoked. Get firm and own what you want. Then you send out a clear signal to the universe, to God, to send you exactly what you want.

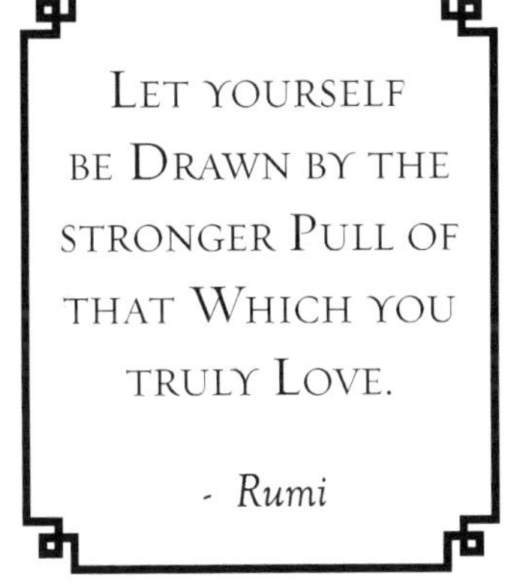

With the written list, I had a road map. If a guy showed up that did not match my list, then I knew without a shadow of a doubt, to move on. We dibble dabble and try to make something happen; we'll make him give up smoking later, for example.

You have to take a guy right where he is when you meet him. If you can't, he's not the one, so move on. We start to rationalize down to a tolerable level. However, love is too important to settle for something you really don't want. This is one area where you don't want second best just because you are lonely and getting older.

You will need to review your list daily to remind yourself of what you truly want. There will be suitors. But you do not have to entertain all suitors. You're in charge and this is your love life, not someone else's.

It is hard to attract love if you are anxious, impatient, and zealous. This is the signal you will project and attract from. If you find yourself continuing to attract the same type of guy, you have to examine the signal you are projecting.

Take a few minutes now, with no restrictions and with no backing down, and write out what you want and what you don't want in the person you want to attract.

Also write down what you have to offer.

> YOUR TASK IS NOT TO SEEK FOR LOVE, BUT MERELY TO SEEK AND FIND ALL THE BARRIERS WITHIN YOURSELF THAT YOU HAVE BUILT AGAINST IT.
>
> *- Rumi*

Remember that whatever you expect from your future love interest, you need to offer the same. For example, if you want someone with a good credit score, make sure your credit is good. If you want someone who is healthy, make sure you are fit and healthy. Got it?

Now, talk the talk and walk the walk. Commit to your list and go about your business being the best you you can be, with a heart that is open and receptive to love. Nothing else even matters except pure love. The type of car he drives, the type of position he holds–unless these are your top priorities, they should not affect your decision to engage with a potential suitor if your dominant values are present.

If your list is filled with external "stuff" and devoid of the true essence of love, then you will most likely attract what you're looking for. Go for the love, if that is what you desire above all. I did and got exactly what I wanted. And now, beyond my wildest dreams, I also enjoy an extension of this love via a little baby boy and a little baby girl. And I thank God for it all.

BARRIERS TO LOVE

I really want you to experience love at a soul-to-soul, essence-to-essence, pure love level. Let's briefly look at a few barriers to love so you can come to terms with where you are and how to move on from here.

Fear

You did all the right things. You found love, maybe married and started a family. Something happened. Divorce, the death of a mate, someone cheated on you, or abused you. You opened yourself completely to love and your heart got broken.

It is all seemingly very difficult. We tend to count these occurrences as bad, unfair, and sad. The truth is, the occurrence is an event. We make it good or bad by the label we ascribe to it. As we stay emotionally connected to the "event," we continue to be underpinned with fear that it will happen again. Therefore, we avoid situations and people that could put us back into a similar situation.

Sometimes this happens subconsciously. Healing a broken heart takes self-healing and time. In the process of self-healing, the main ingredient is forgiveness of one's self as well as the other person. This is the only way you can put yourself back into a position to experience love again.

There are no guarantees in love. Love requires absolute faith. And you have to be "available" to love freely from your soul and receive fully into your soul.

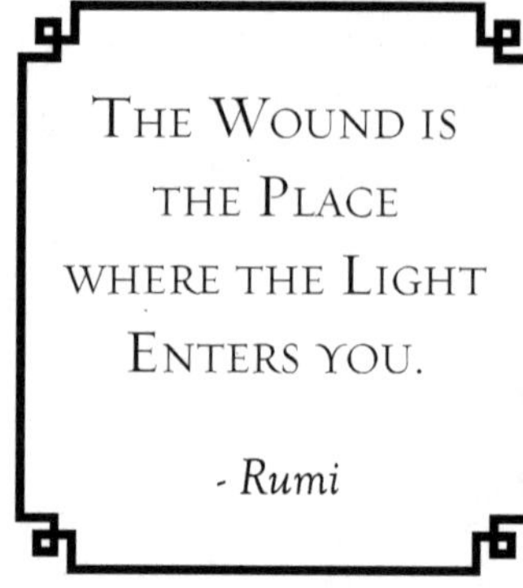

Mistrust

You won't allow yourself to trust anyone and you may not be able to trust yourself and your decisions. The root cause of mistrust relates back to fear. Once you absolve yourself of the fear, then you will be able to trust again. Really, you are simply making a decision to trust and acting in alignment with your conscious decision to trust.

If you seek out or enter into a relationship in a state of mistrust, you will attract someone who will give you cause to mistrust. Regardless of the outcome of any seemingly unfortunate situation, for example if you get hurt again, all things work together for our good (Romans 8:28). There is no situation that you have encountered or will encounter that does not work together for your highest good.

I know that it is a hard walk but you don't have to walk it alone. There are those of us who have done the work and landed on the love spot. It requires trusting and loving fully. Therefore, you have to let go and fly right into the bulls-eye of love, letting go of your fear and mistrust.

Closed

You have closed yourself off to love. You have decided that love is not for you. Maybe your parent or caregiver withheld love from you and it caused you to self-preserve (i.e., keep your heart closed from receiving love to protect it - no love in and no love out). To avoid future hurt, you have sealed your heart off to love. However, love is for everyone and everyone needs love in their life to thrive. It's a well-known fact that babies fail to thrive if they do not receive love and affection. In fact, some infants have died from lack of touch. Again, I encourage you to heal the wounds of your past so you can let your heart be open and receptive to receive the rarest of all gems–pure love.

Perfectionism

You're a high achieving perfectionist. Beautiful, strong, and successful. You've made it and now you're ready for love.

In our "perfect" world, things are supposed to unfold logically. You've worked hard, never letting up. Mr. Right better appear now and "come with everything on my list." Well, let me gently remind you, Mr. Right may not show up exactly as you have planned.

As Rumi, the 13th century Persian theologian, said, *"Lovers don't finally meet somewhere. They're in each other all along."* There is a good chance that your love is actually close by but you can't "see" him because you are wearing your perfectionistic glasses.

While I want you to commit to your list that we talked about above, remember to render the external irrelevant. What you are looking for is true pure love. Love is not of a specific race or economic background. It is not a certain height or weight. Focus on the internal when you are opening yourself up to love and see what possibilities are right under your nose.

Open your eyes, child. The love of my life was only one friend away. That's how close my future husband was to me. But do you know what I thought to myself the second time I met him? "Who does he think he is?" You see, Gary was wearing a ponytail and he didn't have a ponytail the first time I had met him six months prior.

I thought, "What? What guy wears a ponytail?" Well, probably a guy who is very comfortable with who he is. My clean-shaved image of a *suitable* guy caused me to have a strong reaction to his appearance. He now says that I liked that he was his own man, even though I was being a perfectionist about it at the time.

Just think. What if I had let a ponytail keep me from being open to the purest love that I have ever known? I know you won't do this.

Attracting from the False-Version of You

I opened this chapter with a cautionary note: Never attract from the false-version of you. If you have not done so or are in the process of doing your "inner work," please don't engage in pursuing or responding to a love interest. Most likely, you are bound to repeat the past hang-ups that you have experienced that did not end in a true love match. Whatever issue you are working on (trust, self-esteem, perfectionism, unforgiveness, fear, etc.), you will need to take the time, be brave, and really do your "inner work" to overcome your barrier(s) to love.

> LOVE IS AN IRRESISTIBLE DESIRE TO BE IRRESISTIBLY DESIRED.
>
> - *Robert Frost*

The most sacred part of your soul craves a meaningful loving relationship and has the desire to be loving. You also have all the answers deep inside of you. You know when something and someone is good for you and you know when they are not good for you. Trust yourself. You will invariably attract a different kind of love in a freed-up state than if you continue to operate from the false version of you.

In your freed-up state, you are pure love, magnificent and brilliant. The brilliance is what attracts. Love yourself and express love freely. True love is right around the corner.

IF YOU ALREADY HAVE A LOVE IN YOUR LIFE

Value and appreciate the love of your life for the beautiful things about them and all of the beautiful things you have co-created together. Cherish the pure love of their heart. Love them for who they are and who they are becoming. Serve them and help them get to their highest good. Minimize the trivial and focus on and see them through the eyes of God, who sees them as perfection and pure love. Treat him or her with honor and respect, as a King or Queen.

Make yourself more open to love and deal with any unresolved hurt, resentment, and mistrust. Give more of yourself to your love with no expectation for anything in return. This is how you deepen the love you already have.

RENEW DAILY TO STAY FREED-UP

In order to move closer and closer to the love you desire, you must renew "who you are" daily. I mean the freed-up version of you. If circumstances and triggers remind you of the false version of you or try to ensnare you once again, renew your mind (Romans 12:2) to the way you want to be, think, and feel and the type of person and love you want. As you stay conscious of your best self and who you want to enter your life, love will happen.

What do you do while in the waiting game? Live and express more of who you really are. The more you express you out loud and dance with your soul, the less you will be focused on "finding" a love interest and the love interest will find you. When you lose yourself in you and lose yourself in God, you will have pep in your step and your strides will become longer and more alluring.

Trust me, you will begin to radiate and attract. Your voice will change with tones of confidence and definitiveness, not tentativeness and uncertainty. There is so much more in store for you. Remember, too, that there is no limit to your evolving self. Your growth is ever unfolding. There will always be opportunities presented to you to show you where you need to continue to grow in grace and love.

Believe me, love is one area that contains all of life. We are created in love and through the essence of God, who is love. You have every right to desire a wholesome and soul-deep love. Don't give up or get discouraged. Change your mindset and do your work. Love is beautiful and it is for you. When you really do your inner work, remove the barriers and commit to the love you desire and deserve, it will come.

AFFIRMATION

The love I seek is seeking me. I open my heart and I experience love at my deepest soul level.

TIPS AND STRATEGIES TO ATTRACT THE LOVE YOU WANT

- Do the inner work to free yourself from barriers to love. Get freed-up forever.

- Do not enter a relationship until you do the inner work.

- Make a list of your top values in a love interest. Write down those things you don't want. Be honest and real. This is your list and no one else's.

- Commit to your list. Read it every morning and night. Evaluate all suitors against this list. If they don't make the cut - move on.

- Thank God for the love that you expect by faith to enter your life.

- Go about your business living your life on purpose, content and loving God and yourself. Be the best you there is.

- Be the love you seek. Extend yourself in lovingkindness in all that you do.

- Let love radiate out from you 360 degrees. And soon it will radiate to you as you open yourself fully to love.

The chance to love and be loved exists no matter where you are.

-Oprah Winfrey

CHAPTER FOURTEEN

COMMIT TO REST, RETREAT AND RENEW

There is a time for everything, and a season for every activity under the heavens. - Ecclesiastes 3:1, NIV

A TIME TO WORK AND A TIME TO REST

Rest: to stop working for a period of time from your day-to-day activities, calling, mission, etc.

Retreat: to withdraw or take a step back to a remote place or location to reflect, contemplate, and connect on a deeper level to God or your soul's passion. Can be done in solitude or with a community.

Renew: to re-establish your attention to your soul and come back to wholeness.

It is amazing how far you have Come Back to Yourself! In your unending road to your highest self, there will be times when you will need to renew and reconnect to your true self and your true values. You will need to find a sanctuary where you can recalibrate your soul, or reset your soul.[1] It's a time to –

> *. . . Come with me by yourselves to a quiet place and get some rest. Mark 6:31, NIV*

I hope you are incorporating renewal and reconnection every day in order to Practice the Presence of God like we discussed in Chapter 12. This practice will lay the foundation for your rest, retreat, and renewal.

Now we are going to discuss how important it is to regularly take time out to rest and retreat so you can renew, recharge, and reconnect to your soul. Your soul is where your "happy points" reside, whatever gives you immense pleasure, without cognitive or external censors. Another way to describe your soul is that it is the ultimate depths of your being. Your soul is also where your feminine energy resides which includes your–

1) Imagination
2) Passion and Desires
3) Emotions
4) Creativity

Conversely, your masculine energy is made of –

1) Will Power
2) Action and Motivation
3) Intellect
4) Productivity[2]

Guess which one of these our society values and rewards and which one we spend most of our work-life in? You guessed it: masculine energy. However, we need both feminine and masculine energy to be whole. We tend to devalue and suppress our feminine energy, often subconsciously, because we have been socially conditioned to do so. We don't want to appear weak or soft. However, when we neglect the longings in our soul or let our soul hibernate, our soul suffers. Now do you see why we have to intentionally retreat to nurture the feminine aspects of our soul?

I know you get tired. Sometimes you are emotionally drained as well as being physically drained. We discussed in Chapter 11 some chronic conditions that wear down your health. But did you know that going long periods without an explicit rest can lead to burnout? Burnout is when you fizzle out and continually feel drained, which affects your productivity and relationships.

And did you know that chronic stress can eventually cause your body to shut down? I know someone this happened to and they were forced to take time off from work. Well, I'm encouraging you to plan ahead and make time to rest and retreat so this doesn't happen to you.

> HALF AN HOUR'S MEDITATION IS ESSENTIAL EXCEPT WHEN YOU ARE VERY BUSY. THEN A FULL HOUR IS NEEDED.
>
> *- Saint Francis de Sales*

Because we have so many aspects to our lives, we can become fragmented, getting further and further away from our soul's longing. When we become fragmented, we are torn between many different directions and lose our effectiveness.

Because you are on a road to greatness, you must proactively plan to "retreat" Back to Yourself, to recalibrate your soul and return to wholeness.

And the very God of peace sanctify you wholly; and I pray God your whole spirit and soul and body be preserved blameless unto the coming of our Lord Jesus Christ.
-1 Thessalonians 5:23, KJV

Your soul is the essence of your being. Your spirit is your divine passageway to connect and commune with God, who is Spirit (John 4:24), and your body holds your spirit and soul. All three elements require you to rest, retreat, and renew.

Before we retreat though, let's remember to be thankful and grateful that we have enough "stimulus" to retreat from and that we know or we are learning the importance of retreating (and that we are going to make the decision to do it!). Please don't short-change this step in your journey to greatness. It is not an add-on; it is as essential as any other part of the actual work.

You remember that my cousin Barbara Jean once told me I was borrowing future time because I was working so hard, so feverishly. (That was before I came to myself when I was a "sprint runner" - running from the child sexual abuse.) While you are young and healthy, it's easy to do it without even thinking about the future consequences. And my dear "Ma,'" the late Pauline Davis, would always tell me (and some of you have already heard this from your elders): "You're so busy, you're like a cat covering up sh*t." Both of my female relatives were right.

BARRIERS TO REST, RETREAT, AND RENEW

You

You are the primary barrier to taking a rest, a retreat to renew and reconnect to your true self. As of this writing, I have not taken a retreat with the intention to rest and renew since BC (before children). Sure, I have gone away for conferences, weddings, and family visits, but this is not what I am talking about. I'm talking about taking a retreat specifically designed for you to reconnect to your whole self.

We have become good at combining work conferences with a couple days of rest and relaxation and we think we're doing something. But how long does it take you to "come down" from a conference before vacationing? Plass and Cofield call this phenomenon being "busy-brained," where your brain is so addicted to thinking, planning, analyzing, and anticipating that it requires some time before you can turn it off and start a true period of rest.[3]

You will need to be intentional about calming your mind down before you can be present for your period of rest. Yes, people save money by combining work and vacation, but we are also coming up to a higher level, right? Now is the time to plan ahead for your next retreat minus the "conference."

Money

One of the barriers to taking a retreat is the appearance of a lack of money. Here's the truth: We find ways to come up with the money for the things we truly want. Think about the benefits to your health, peace of mind, renewed energy to accomplish greater things that a retreat will bring. There are also costs to not renewing yourself: fatigue, chronic stress, depletion, etc. I have also already discussed health ramifications in Chapter 11.

Time

This is the same principle as the money. We make time for the things that truly matter to us and for the people who matter to us. There are 52 weeks in a year. Could you take a 3-day retreat or a 7-day retreat at some point in the year? That leaves you 50+

weeks for work and other activities, as well as more periods of rest. You could possible take a ½ day off from your business or work and go to a movie, go for a swim, get a massage, etc. We have to commit to taking the time to renew.

Guilt

I realize that many individuals experience guilt when you finally commit to putting yourself first. The look on your baby's or puppy's face as you head off to the airport might be just enough for you to call it quits.

When I have to go out of town on business, I try to prepare my kids as best I can to bring them into my pending experience. They often want to know where I will be staying, who I will be talking to, and the like.

I also call in the reinforcements, like Nana, to host a sleepover with the kids as a way to provide a special time for them while I'm gone. I also let the kids know that I will be bringing them something special back so they have something to look forward to. So even when the little tears start to fall down their faces, it doesn't deter me from doing what I have to do.

Those same tactics can be used when you're leaving for a personal retreat. Don't attach any energy to the feelings associated with guilt. Just notice them and put them on a leaf and let them float down the river bend and you get on the plane and retreat!

Technology

How in the world could you ever go without checking your emails and voicemails, texting, tweeting, and instagramming? Well, you can. You have to make the decision to shut down the technology in exchange for recalibrating your soul.

In case of a true emergency, give a couple of close friends and family members the number where you're staying so they can reach you on the telephone. Otherwise, make a commitment not to check emails or voicemails or texts. Recently, I went away to a women's conference and for five days I never once looked at my email. I surprised myself, but it was incredibly freeing.

RECOMMIT TO DANCING WITH YOUR SOUL AND EXPLORING YOUR DEEPER PASSIONS

As we become more successful in fulfilling our purpose and mission, we often lose sight of the people and experiences that cause us to dance with our soul. As we discussed in Chapter 5, whatever feeds your soul, do more of it, mindfully.

Is there a retreat for dancing with your soul? If golf creates the dancing with your soul effect, go on a golf retreat. If dancing ignites your soul, take a dance cruise. If it's jazz music, how about a jazz cruise? If yoga is your thing, there are plenty of yoga retreats. The idea here is whatever you identify as dancing with your soul, take time away and do more of that activity on a deeper, more concentrated level.

Have you ever considered taking a spa retreat to rejuvenate your mind, body, and soul? There are day, destination, hot tub, cruise ship, and even mobile spas–services that are brought to you. The purpose of a spa retreat is to refocus on your overall health and well-being. Some spas also focus on nourishing the body through healthy eating and seminars on nutrition. (Check the Resources page for a link to a list of all types of available retreats.)

Here's one for you: Rest also means taking time to renew your faith and commune with God outside of the day-to-day cares of this world. Have you ever considered taking a spiritual or meditation retreat? Wow! The main purpose of this type of retreat is to quiet the mind and tune out the external for a period of time dedicated to seeking a deeper connection to God. There are also many spiritual retreats beginning with those in your own community and stretching to faraway places such as Hawaii.

Have you ever considered taking a spiritual sabbatical? The authors, Plass and Cofield defined this type of sabbatical as a period of rest from all ministry, missions, and work-related tasks. It can include retreating to a different geographic region to allow God to penetrate the deepest part of your soul by spending time listening to Him, reflecting on His goodness, and asking soul-searching questions such as, "What really matters to me at this point in my life?"

How many people do you know who have ever taken a spiritual sabbatical? I've always heard that great people spend significant time with God. This is a wonderful opportunity for you and it is not by accident that you are reading this paragraph right now.

> COMMIT YOUR WORK TO THE LORD, AND YOUR PLANS WILL SUCCEED.
>
> *- Proverbs 16:3 CEB*

Go online and start searching for spas, yoga retreats, spiritual retreats, etc. Become familiar with their offerings and then start to look into the prices. The more you go in the direction you want, the sooner you will get there. Henry David Thoreau told us that "... if one advances confidently in the direction of his dreams, and endeavors to live the life which he has imagined, he will meet with a success unexpected in common hours." Start a savings plan for your next retreat.

I can't wait to hear about your retreat. Please share your experience with me at http://www.chaneldeguzman.com.

It would not be difficult to keep going, finishing up just one more project or assignment. Remember that you are at a new level; you are becoming the greatest expression of you. Therefore, you have will to take charge and build in time to rest, retreat and renew.

No one around you is going to make this a priority for you. People, employers, business partners, family members are happy to see you "doing," especially if they benefit.

Be more purposeful in your commitment to take a break. Your body, spirit and soul will be revived to reengage more calm, centered, and refreshed. You're worth it! Your soul longs to steal away. What are you waiting for?

AFFIRMATION

I am committed to take the time to rest, retreat, and renew and I feel at peace and exceedingly well.

TIPS AND STRATEGIES TO REST, RETREAT AND RENEW

- Take a Spa day
- Plan a weekend get-away
- Take a Gratitude Walk (walking while noticing opportunities to express gratitude)
- Get a hot stone massage

- Sleep/Nap
- Open a designated account to save for your retreat (e.g. Spa Retreat Fund)
- Create a vision board of your ideal retreat
- Visualize in your mind what you are dreaming of for your retreat. Imagine what you will be doing on your retreat and how you will feel
- Consider taking a spiritual sabbatical to recalibrate your soul and commune with God
- Commit your retreating plans to God
- At a minimum, take a one-minute mini-retreat daily: stop working and take three conscious breaths, enjoy a sip of water and give thanks.

Each of us needs to withdraw from the cares which will not withdraw from us. We need hours of aimless wandering or spates of time sitting on park benches, observing the mysterious world of ants and the canopy of treetops.

-Maya Angelou

CHAPTER FIFTEEN

LEAVE AN IMPACT AND A LEGACY

Create your legacy by fulfilling your potential.
-Gino Norris

Wow. We have made it to the end, to your legacy. Do you realize that you have much to impart to others and you get to decide what legacy you will leave? This feels so exciting, and yet somehow daunting at the same time.

To whom much is given, much is required (Luke 12:48). There is both power and responsibility afforded with the gifts, talents, and knowledge entrusted to us. Let's be faithful with the power that lies within us.

Leaving a legacy means you are putting your stamp, your imprint on the world and on the future. Your legacy lives beyond your lifetime and is carried forward by your descendants, your tribe, and/or your community.

Think beyond where you are today. You might be thinking, "I don't need to leave a legacy. I'm just stepping into my own greatness. Do I really need to be thinking about a legacy? Can't I just wait until I'm older?"

We tend to think we have an unlimited amount of time on this earth. However, according to the Centers for Disease Control and Prevention, the US life expectancy for women in 2012 was 81.2 years of age (76.4 for men).[1] So you can conclude that the average woman is reaching middle-age around 40ish. Geesh. We'd better get busy. But even if you're well over 40, that doesn't mean it's too late for you. However, it does mean it's time to get started.

Leaving a legacy ensures that others you care about will inherit the knowledge of how to be whole and free and will know the everlasting, eternal God. These beneficiaries will also carry on the causes that are most meaningful to you.

The world continues to hurt and be in need. Enlightened people like you help change the world for the better for the generations who follow by taking responsibility and deliberately leaving a legacy and a "how to" manual. Let's get started and decide what your legacy will be.

> Therefore I say unto you, what things soever ye desire, when ye pray, believe that ye receive them, and ye shall have them.
>
> *- Mark 11:24, KJV*

DEFINE YOUR IMPACT AND LEGACY

First, start with the end in mind. We spent a good amount of time in Chapter 6 defining our vision based on what is most meaningful to us. In defining your impact and legacy, we want to take this definition further, now looking from the perspective that we have actually arrived. We are now "gifting" our legacy to future generations.

> A Good person Leaves an Inheritance for their Children's children.
>
> *- Proverbs 13:22, NIV*

Think about the process you have hopefully gone through planning your estate. Guided by your trusted legal counselor, you identified which entities and people (often your children) you wanted to leave portions of your estate to (yes, we all have estates, just to varying degrees).

During a meeting where our attorney reviewed our actual estate plan with us, there was a provision we made to have our children's children provided for, in case our children die before their children. My husband and I thought how incredible it is that generations will receive something of value because of our deliberate planning today. Likewise, this is why you want to proactively plan the legacy you will leave, even though it's rather intangible in nature.

Please take some time to thoughtfully reflect on what legacy you would like to design and what impact your presence will have in this world. You will need to use your creative, freed-up mind to envision beyond where you are today and grow your legacy as you grow.

Here are a few questions to get you thinking:

- What is the most meaningful aspect of my life?

- What matters to me more than anything in the world?

- What causes and organizations share my vision that I really care about?
- How will I communicate and share my passion?
- What is the most pressing problem in the world that I want to see fixed?
- What gets me angry? (This area will show you where you can have impact to solve the very thing that gets you angry.)
- What difference will I make?
- What can I do to make those around me more successful?
- Which group of people am I compelled to make a difference with? (e.g., young, elderly, vulnerable, boys, girls, women, men, hungry, afflicted, abused, homeless, orphaned, talented, etc.)

Take some time right now to write down your legacy, drawing from your responses to these reflective questions.

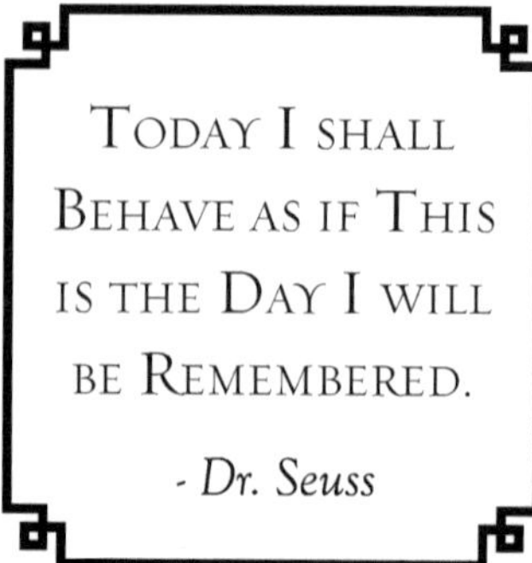

As you continue to grow and become all you were meant to be, as defined by you, you will need to revisit your legacy so that it is always well beyond where you are at any given point in time. Keep reading and you will have a chance to bring all the elements of your legacy together at the end of this chapter.

LIVE LIFE WITH A LEGACY ORIENTATION

Once you have become clear on the impact and legacy you want to have, you will need to start to live it out daily, through your actions, and communicate it verbally and in written form as often as you can. There should be no doubt, to yourself and others, as to what you stand for. All roads lead back to your legacy.

Keep a journal of how you live out your impact and legacy daily. You will have to become mindful of your legacy in order to walk it out and build it. You will need to experience a mind shift so you are conscious of your legacy in your day-to-day interactions with those around you and with those whom you want to impact.

One way that may help you live your daily life with a legacy orientation is to think in terms of being an ambassador or a diplomat, for example a Colin Powell type.

Colin Powell is a retired statesman and four-star general who became the Country's first African American Secretary of State and the Chairman of the Joint Chiefs of Staff. He devoted his entire adult life to public service and during his retirement co-founded the American's Promise Alliance, along with his wife, to develop "character and confidence" in youth from all socioeconomic backgrounds. The organization has a presence in more than 500 communities in all 50 states.[2] The key elements of his legacy are that he serves and has tremendous impact on youth. His legacy is a process of leadership, of moving from a warrior who fights and defends to an ambassador who is poised under pressure, serves his country and leaves an impact.

YOUR SPIRITUAL LEGACY

While it seems obvious to most of us that we would pass down our wealth through our estate planning as I described, I don't think we are mindful of passing down the intangible aspects of our spiritual knowledge and gifts–of all that God has invested in us–to our kids, loved ones, and those we care about.

You can genuinely transfer your knowledge and values from a place of wholeness because of the inner work you have done. You also have a special vantage point because of your heart-to-heart connection with your loved ones. Your legacy is the seed to another's spiritual growth and development. However, he or she is ultimately responsible to nurture the seed and grow their own faith.

> THE CHOICES WE MAKE ABOUT THE LIVES WE LIVE DETERMINE THE KINDS OF LEGACIES WE LEAVE.
>
> *- Tavis Smiley*

You probably are already imparting your faith to your children and those around you, but maybe you did not realize you are leaving a faith legacy: one that conveys your belief in God to your descendants, co-workers, community, and family.

When you really know a person, you know what they stand for, who they stand for, and why. So what would the people closest to you say that you stand for? Who would they say you stand for? And why?

PRISTINE LEGACY OR TARNISHED LEGACY

Perhaps another way to think about legacy is through your reputation. Live in such a way that your reputation precedes you. Keep your legacy pristine.

When my younger sister died in a truck accident, I was a doctoral student at Wayne State University in Detroit. My two nieces, who were also involved in the accident, survived, but spent several months in intensive care. After spending about a month at the hospital with my nieces, I finally left the hospital and started resuming various aspects of my life.

The first day I planned to go back to school, I stopped by to see my professor to reconnect with her and to see how she recommended I get back into the classroom and make up the work. Her response went something like this: Chanel, they will eat you up in class. They'll want to know everything that happened, the condition of the girls, etc. I don't want you to have to relive all of that. I am giving you an "A" for the course because your reputation precedes you.

I could not believe what I was hearing. There were two months left in the course. I had missed over a month of material and my professor was allowing me to rest on my laurels? No incomplete grade, no making up assignments and missed tests. I was blown away.

Well, I accepted the blessing for what it was and I learned a valuable lesson about a reputation. Whether we realize it or not, everything we say and do affects our reputation and adds to our legacy. All of our interactions, seen or not seen, are some of the building blocks that shape our legacy.

When I think of examples of legacy these are the "forces" that come to mind:

- President Barack Obama
- Oprah Winfrey
- Bill and Melinda Gates
- Warren Buffet
- Maya Angelou

They are more than "legends." Legends can do it all. But when legends leave, a monumental gap exists because they did not grow others to fill the gap.

The individuals I have referenced above have made indelible marks in the world and are concerned about developing others to become major players in the arenas they are a part of. Think of Oprah Winfrey's Life Class through which she shares life-changing principles with millions of people. She is making a significant impact and building a legacy.

Now, let's look at the flipside of a pristine legacy–a tarnished legacy. I was sitting in a courtroom one day, waiting patiently to present my case to the judge, challenging a parking violation ticket I believed I received in error.

I sat and sat and sat some more. Each case I heard was more or less the same: Do you know the charges against you? Please tell the court what happened the night you were pulled over. Then the defendant's attorney would tell the judge that this person comes from "good stock," works or goes to school, and would the judge please extend leniency.

> EVEN A CHILD IS KNOWN BY HIS DOINGS, WHETHER HIS WORK BE PURE, AND WHETHER IT BE RIGHT.
>
> *- Proverbs 20:11, ASV*

Each person's case was textbook: same lingo, fees, and penalties. Each person's talk ended with a sincere apology to the judge, offering a vow never to be seen in that judge's court again. Some defendants had lawyers and some represented themselves.

All of the people in this courtroom were standing before the judge because they were caught driving under the influence of alcohol.

It was amazing to me that these individuals were about as diverse a group as I had ever seen:

middle-aged professional women, grandfathers, young adults, varying racial and socioeconomic backgrounds. But they all had the same story: "I normally don't do this but this is what happened..."

Finally after about an hour of seeing me seated there, the Bailiff, while escorting one of the defendants out of the courtroom to pay their court fees said, "You don't belong here. Where do you need to be?" I told him I was trying to challenge a ticket. He said, "I thought so. I knew you didn't belong in this courtroom." We both chuckled a little. I have to say, I did overlook his stereotyping of me and chalked it up to him being very experienced in handling "his" courtroom and his pre-judgment could tell that that courtroom was not the place for me.

I thought how sad that these individuals got caught up in this type of activity, which was probably not their first occurrence, but perhaps the first time they got caught. This was a small community, too.

Can you imagine if you had a pristine reputation and now it has become tarnished by making a perilous choice? Well, we do see this played out on the big stage. There are a few individuals who come to mind whose legacy, some that we watched for a lifetime, have been instantly tarnished and wiped out:

Bill Cosby has got to be one that typifies the enormity of having a strong, vibrant living legacy and then having it tarnished due to illegal behavior (he admitted to putting sedatives in women's drinks, without their knowledge, with whom he had intended to have sex).[3] Dr. Cosby seemed to have spent a lifetime admonishing the African American race to strive and achieve and he invested millions into historically black colleges, most of whom have disavowed their association with him.[4] A number of entities have severed ties with Cosby, including Walt Disney World in Orlando, Florida, where his statue was removed.

Here are a few more names that come to mind when I think of people whose legacy became tarnished:

- Pete Rose
- Charlie Sheen
- Senator John Edwards
- Joe Paterno

We all need to be mindful of the importance of our legacy. It can be diminished no matter who you are.

Therefore do not let what you know is good be spoken of as evil. - Romans 14:16, NIV

Your legacy reflects your whole life, and you will be remembered mostly for what you have contributed to the world–especially where you touched lives through genuine love and helped others become successful.

Here's the legacy I want to leave:

That my kids know the love of God at their soul and spirit levels. That I touched millions of lives by providing transformative content that helped people to be whole and free. That I influenced girls to be educated, stand in their power, and delay having babies until they are in-love married and truly ready.

I have fought the good fight. I have finished my course, I have kept the faith. - 2 Timothy 4:7, KJV

AFFIRMATION

I inspire and empower others to greatness through my legacy.

TIPS AND STRATEGIES FOR IMPACT AND LEGACY

- Define your legacy using your creative, freed-up mind.
- Declare and decree and be mindful of your legacy daily.
- Live your life in a manner that leads to a legacy you're proud of.
- Keep a journal of how you live out your impact and legacy daily.
- Create a vision board with images that depict your legacy. Visualize the images with a feeling of accomplishment every morning and night.
- Create measurable goals that stem from your legacy statement.

- Reflect on your legacy to determine if you are actively helping the people around you be successful.
- Revise your legacy as you reach higher heights in your growth.

No matter what happens in life, be good to people. Being good to people is the best legacy you can leave behind.

-The #438 Rule of a Lady

WELCOME BACK!

You have been on an amazing journey. You are a completely different person than you were when you first started this book. And now you're well on your way to living a totally amazing life . . . the life you were created to live.

I know it can sometimes be painful to look back at where you once were, but it can also be encouraging. Especially when you've made such outstanding progress.

Not too long ago you were a false version of yourself. You had forgotten who you are, what you really want, and how much greatness God had deposited inside you.

Now you're REAL. And you're confident in the real you. You're beginning to fulfill the great purpose you were put on this earth to do.

You are no longer waiting for anyone else to make your life valuable, to tell you who you are, or to pay you back for anything they've taken from you. You've forgiven everyone–including yourself–and you do whatever it takes to keep it that way.

The life you're learning to live is lived on purpose, focused on fulfilling the new vision you have for your life and not wasting your time on anyone else's agendas.

You're taking care of your body and your spirit and you are allowing your innate brilliance to shine through in every situation–with no apologies.

You are bravely facing each challenge that comes to you, looking for the lesson that's included, and learning that lesson quickly so you're ready to pursue the next venture it's preparing you for.

Your accomplishments are not dependent on anyone else. You know you were created with everything you need to successfully live the life God created you to live.

And that's what you're doing.

But you also need to know that nothing you ever do will make God love you any more and nothing you fail to do will make Him love you any less. He just loves you! And in response, you can show your love for Him by enjoying this amazing life He's given you.

My prayer is that you'll daily do the work required to continue to Love Life and Live Free . . . now that you've ***Come Back To Yourself!***

Well done, my good and faithful servant.
- Matthew 25:21, NLT

Give thanks in everything, for this is God's will for you in Christ Jesus. - 1 Thessalonians 5:18, HCSB

ACKNOWLEDGEMENTS

First, I want to thank God and My Lord and Savior, Jesus Christ, who kept me during this project and is my all in all and the essence of who I am–love.

This book would not be here without my coach, Geoffrey Berwind. You work as hard as I do in each coaching session. Thank you for praying with me, always. Thank you for being there with me, every step of the way.

A special thank you to Steve Harrison and to Martha Bullen, my writing coach. Thank you to Anne Jolles, who had the divine insight to suggest and encourage me take a sabbatical to write.

Thank you to my best editor, Rhonda Fleming. You walked beside me every step of the way. You encouraged me through it all. Thank you from all of my heart.

Thank you to Jerry Dorris for my front cover design. I appreciate you.

And to my graphic designer and sister-friend, LaTanya Orr, who has been around this track three times. Third time was the charm. Thank you for always being there when I was ready to go.

To all of the women and men I referenced in this book, thank you for being willing to show your vulnerabilities and strength to me.

To my Mom for my life, who is always proud of me and lives vicariously through me. Thank you for your unfailing love.

And a special thank you to my children, Gian and Giavanni, for your love and understanding while Mommy was "always" away writing. I love you.

And to the only man who can handle it all, Gary DeGuzman, my love: All The Time! I love you!

NOTES

CHAPTER 3: YOUR SECRET PAIN

1. Marianne Williamson, A Woman's Worth, New York: Random House, 1994.

2. Russ Harris, The Confidence Gap: A Guide to Overcoming Fear and Self-Doubt, Boston: Trumpeter Books, 2011.

3. Joe Dispenza, Breaking the Habit of Being Yourself: How to Lose Your Mind and Create a New One, New York: Hay House, Inc., 2012, p. 168.

4. Dispenza, Breaking the Habit, p. 168.

5. Dispenza, Breaking the Habit, p. 102.

CHAPTER 4: UNFORGIVENESS

1. "Fetzer Survey on Love and Forgiveness in American Society," Fetzer Institute, http://fetzer.org/resources/fetzer-survey-love-and-forgiveness-american-society.

2. Jessica Marie Schultz, "Does forgiveness matter? A study of spiritual transformation among survivors of significant interpersonal offenses," PhD (Doctor of Philosophy) thesis, University of Iowa, 2011, http://ir.uiowa.edu/cgi/viewcontent.cgi?article=2560&context=etd.

3. "The Deadly Consequences of Unforgiveness," Lorie Johnson, Last modified June 22, 2015, http://www1.cbn.com/cbnnews/healthscience/2015/June/The-Deadly-Consequences-of-Unforgiveness/.

4. "Forgiveness: Your Health Depends On It," Johns Hopkins Medicine, accessed December 14, 2015, http://www.hopkinsmedicine.org/health/healthy_aging/healthy_connections/forgiveness-your-health-depends-on-it.

CHAPTER 5: DANCE WITH YOUR SOUL

1. "Gallup Poll: 70% of Americans Hate Their Stupid Jobs," RYOT, Last modified January 10, 2013, http://www.ryot.org/gallup-poll-70-americans-disengaged-jobs/376177.

CHAPTER 6: CREATE YOUR VISION, MISSION AND VALUES

1. "The Most Popular Talks of all Time," TED, http://www.ted.com/playlists/171/the_most_popular_talks_of_all.

2. "Short Biography: Mother Teresa of Calcutta (1910-1997)," Mother Teresa of Calcutta Center Official Cite, http://www.motherteresa.org.

3. "The Complete Worksheets for The Confidence Gap," Russ Harris, http://www.thehappinesstrap.com/free_resources.

4. Ken Blanchard, Leading at a Higher Level: Blanchard on Leadership and Creating High Performing Organizations, New Jersey: FT Press, 2007, p. 264.

5. "Job Postings," Mercy Sioux City, Accessed November 1, 2015, http://www.mercysiouxcity.com/job-postings.

CHAPTER 7: DEVELOP YOUR POWER, PRESENCE AND VOICE

1. Bill Cropper, Personal Mastery – Putting the 'Me' in Leadership, http://www.thechangeforum.com/Personal_Mastery.htm.

2. Lou Tice, Imagine 21 ~ Fast Track to Change Video Resource Guide, Seattle: The Pacific Institute, 1999.

3. Russ Harris, The Confidence Gap: A Guide to Overcoming Fear and Self-Doubt, Boston: Trumpeter Books, 2011.

4. Russ Harris, The Confidence Gap, p. 235.

5. Kristi Hedges, The Power of Presence: Unlock Your Potential: Unlock Your Potential to Influence and Engage Others, New York: AMACO, 2012.

6. "Are You Giving Your Power Away? Time to reclaim it!" Elari Onawa, http://elarionawa.com/personal-power.

7. "How You Give Your Power Away," Steve Pavlina, February 2, 2010,http://www.stevepavlina.com/blog/2010/02/how-you-give-your-power-away/.

8. Russ Harris, The Confidence Gap, p. 198.

CHAPTER 8: MENTOR FOR SUCCESS

1. "6 Things You Must Do to Be a Great Mentor and Leader," John Murphy, The Undercover Recruiter, http://theundercoverrecruiter.com/be-great-mentor-leader.

2. Audrey J. Murrel, "Five Key Steps for Effective Mentoring Relationship," The Kaitz Quarterly, Volume 1, No.1, Washington DC, 2007.

CHAPTER 9: UNVEIL YOUR BRILLIANCE

1. Tia Goodwin, Girlfriend, It's Your Time!: Reclaim Your Brilliance and Step Into Your Purpose, Westbow Press, 2014.

2. Joe Dispenza, Breaking the Habit of Being Yourself: How to Lose Your Mind and Create a New One, New York: Hay House, Inc., 2012, p. 146.

CHAPTER 10: DISCOVER NEW TRAILS FOR GROWTH

1. Nevitt Sanford, The American College, New York: Wiley, 1982.

2. "Grow Bigger Than Your Problems, T. Harv Eker, http://www.abundance-and-happiness.com/t-harv-eker-grow-bigger-than-your-problems.html.

3. Lou Tice, Imagine 21 ~ Fast Track to Change Video Resource Guide, Seattle: The Pacific Institute, 1999.

CHAPTER 11: MAINTAIN HEALTH AND WELLNESS

1. "The Importance of Staying Fit and Healthy, Thriving and Finding Balance at 50," Huffington Post, Last updated August 10, 2014, http://www.huffingtonpost.com/mark-and-debbie-abbott/the-importance-of-staying-fit-healthy-thriving-finding-balance-at-50_b_5447183.html.

2. "What Is Personal Mastery?" HubPages, Updated February 6, 2010, http://hubpages.com/business/what-is-personal-mastery-2

3. Joe Dispenza, Breaking the Habit of Being Yourself: How to Lose Your Mind and Create a New One, New York: Hay House, Inc., 2012, p.99.

4. "Physical Activity Improves Quality of Life," American Heart Association, Last reviewed January 2015, http://www.heart.org/HEARTORG/HealthyLiving/PhysicalActivity/StartWalking/Physical-activity-improves-quality-of-life_UCM_307977_Article.jsp#.VqGMR_krKUm.

5. "Do You Know Some of the Health Risks of Being Overweight?" Institute of Diabetes and Digestive and Kidney Diseases, Updated December, 2012, http://www.niddk.nih.gov/health-information/health-topics/weight-control/health_risks_being_overweight/Pages/health-risks-being-overweight.aspx#a.

6. "About Adult BMI," Center for Disease Control and Prevention, Last updated May 15, 2015, http://www.cdc.gov/healthyweight/assessing/bmi/adult_bmi/index.html#Definition.

7. "How Accurate Is Body Mass Index, or BMI?" WebMD, http://www.webmd.com/diet/how-accurate-body-mass-index-bmi?page=2.

8. "Preventing Weight Gain," Center for Disease Control and Prevention, Last updated May 15, 2015, http://www.cdc.gov/healthyweight/prevention.

9. "2008 Physical Activity Guidelines for Americans Summary," Office of Disease Prevention and Health Promotion, http://health.gov/paguidelines/guidelines/summary.

10. Dan Buettner, "The Blue Zones Solution: Eating and Living Like the World's Healthiest People," National Geographic Society, Washington, DC, 2015.

CHAPTER 12: PRACTICE HIS PRESENCE

1. David Martyn Lloyd-Jones, God's Ultimate Purpose: An Exposition of Ephesians 1:1, Grand Rapids, Michigan: Baker Books, 1978, p. 342.

2. "Living in the Presence of God," Fr. John A. Hardon, http://www.therealpresence.org/eucharst/intro/livingpg.htm.

3. "Be in Constant Communion with God," Rick Warren, Last Updated May 21, 2014, http://rickwarren.org/devotional/english/be-in-constant-communion-with-god.

CHAPTER 14: COMMIT TO REST, RETREAT AND RENEW

1. "Refresh & Recalibrate Pt 1: A Divine Reset for Your Soul," Joanna Weaver, Last updated January 6, 2016, http://joannaweaverbooks.com/2016/01/06/refresh-recalibrate-pt-1-a-divine-reset.

2. "How to Heal Your Soul," Wiki How, http://www.wikihow.com/Heal-Your-Soul.

3. Richard Plass and James Cofield, The Relational Soul: Moving from False Self to Deep Connection, Illinois: InterVarsity Press, 2014.

CHAPTER 15: LEAVE AN IMPACT AND A LEGACY

1. "Mortality in the United States, 2012," Jiaquan Xu, M.D.; Kenneth D. Kochanek, M.A.; Sherry L. Murphy, B.S.; Elizabeth Arias, Ph.D., Last updated October 8, 2014, http://www.cdc.gov/nchs/data/databriefs/db168.htm.

2. "Colin Powell Biography," Biography.com, http://www.biography. com/people/colin-powell-9445708.

3. "How Bill Cosby's Fortune and Legacy Collapsed," Daniel Bukszpan, Updated July 15, 2015, http://fortune.com/2015/07/15/bill-cosby-fortune-collapse.

4. "Historically Black Woman's College Severs Ties with Bill Cosby," Sheryl Estrada, Updated July 31, 2015, http://www.diversityinc.com/news/historically-black-womens-college-severs-ties-with-bill-cosby.

RESOURCES

MEDITATION RESOURCES

See: https://www.youtube.com/watch?v=9h4GiblYrPk
Rest and Renew in Dr. Joe Dispenza's Space Free Guided Meditation ~ Monday Meditations

See http://marc.ucla.edu/body.cfm?id=22
Free Guided Meditations by UCLA Mindful Awareness Research Center

See http://herohealthroom.com/2014/12/08/free-guided-meditation-resources/12 of the Best Free Guided Meditation Sites (Updated)

Chapter 6: Create Your Vision, Mission and Values
See http://www.thehappinesstrap.com/free_resources and click on the link entitled, "The Complete Worksheets for The Confidence Gap," for an exhaustive list of values.

Chapter 8: Mentor for Success
See http://business.financialpost.com/executive/leadership/every-great-leader-needs-a-mentor-which-are-you, for help finding the right mentor for you.

Chapter 10: Discover New Trails for Growth
Brian Tracy, How the Best Leaders Lead: Proven Secrets to Getting the Most Out of Yourself and Others, New York: AMACO, 2010.

T. Harv Eker, Secrets Of The Millionaire Mind: Mastering the Inner Game of Wealth, New York: Harper Collins Publishers, 2005.

Chapter 11: Maintain Health and Wellness
See http://www.webmd.com/diet/body-bmi-calculator for a BMI calculator.

Dan Buettner, The Blue Zones Solution: Eating and Living Like the World's Healthiest People, Washington, DC: National Geographic Society, 2015.

Chapter 12: Practice His Presence

4 Steps to Self-Actualization and Becoming the Best Version of You," Kay R. Green, Last updated March 19, 2013, http://www.huffingtonpost.com/r-kay-green/personal-development_b_2479253.html.

Chapter 13: Attract the Love You Want

Dedicate or rededicate your life and heart to God the Father. If you need to, speak with you spiritual leader about this decision. Or you can pray one of these simple prayers from your heart.

Chapter 14: Commit to Rest, Retreat and Renew

See https://en.wikipedia.org/wiki/Spa for a complete listing of the different types of spas.

See http://www.healingholidays.co.uk/blog/how-to-choose-a-spa/guide-to-different-types-of-spas for a complete listing of the different type of spas.

The Prayer of Salvation
Pray this prayer, from your heart to God's heart:

Dear God,

I come to You in the Name of Jesus. I admit that I am not right with You, and I want to be right with You. I ask You to forgive me of all my sins. The Bible says if I confess with my mouth that "Jesus is Lord," and believe in my heart that God raised Him from the dead, I will be saved (Rom. 10:9). I believe with my heart and I confess with my mouth that Jesus is the Lord and Savior of my life. Thank You for saving me!

In Jesus' Name I pray. Amen.

The Prayer of Rededication
(recommitting your life back to Jesus Christ):

If we confess our sins, he is faithful and just to forgive us our sins and to cleanse us from all unrighteousness.
- 1 John 1:9, ESV

Pray this prayer heart to heart to God:

Father, I rededicate my life and heart to you now. Forgive me of my sins as I turn away from them and back to you. Fill me with your love. Pour your love into the deepest part of my soul. Allow the love that you have for me to permeate my entire being. Let this same love extend from me to everyone that I come in contact with. And so it is. Amen.

ABOUT THE AUTHOR

Chanel F. DeGuzman, PhD, holds a Bachelor of Arts degree from the University of Michigan. She earned two Master's degrees concurrently in college student personnel and guidance and counseling from Bowling Green University, and obtained a Doctorate degree in curriculum and instruction from Wayne State University.

Dr. DeGuzman is the founding Director of the University of Michigan Alumni Career Center. She was the Project Director for the Sellers' Lab on Racial Identity in the Department of Psychology, and Director of Academic Diversity Initiatives for the School of Public Health at the University of Michigan.

She has coached women from all walks of life and counseled hundreds of students to realize all the good and greatness inside of them. Her engaging presence and unique training style have inspired audiences to action, including women's organizations, corporations, and academia. She often speaks and leads workshops on leadership, personal mastery, and loving life and living free. Her travels include Scotland, Prague, Brussels, Hawaii, Budapest, Jamaica, Germany and multiple U.S. cities.

She serves on the Advisory Board for Girls Group of Ann Arbor and Board of Directors of Daughter of Beauty - Son of Valor of Bloomfield Hills, the Assistant Treasurer for the Board of Directors for God Land Unity Church in Detroit, and serves on the Executive Board and as the Chaplain for the Ann Arbor (MI) Chapter of the Links, Incorporated.

Dr. DeGuzman is especially excited about her forthcoming book, ***The Forgotten Power of Man***, to be released later in 2016.

When not writing, speaking, coaching, and traveling, Dr. DeGuzman loves being at home with her husband and loves to lavish her two children, Gian and Giavanni, with love and affection. She practices Bikram yoga, is a competitive ballroom dancer, and a "loud" tennis player. She can be contacted at www.chaneldeguzman.com.

CONTACT DR. DeGUZMAN

Speaking

Dr. DeGuzman speaks frequently on the topics of leadership, women's empowerment, and personal mastery. She can deliver a keynote, half-day, or full-day version of this content, based on your needs. If you are interested in finding out more, please visit her Speaking page at www.chaneldeguzman.com/speaking.

Coaching

Dr. DeGuzman offers personal coaching. She will take the time to get to know you, your story, and develop an action plan that is unique to your challenges and desires. She provides solutions to help you let go of what's holding you back, surrender your secret pain through the power of forgiveness, and become freed-up to pursue your highest purpose. If you would like to work with her, sign up at her website at www.chaneldeguzman.com/coaching.

Next Book: **THE FORGOTTEN POWER OF MAN**

Sign up to be notified when Dr. DeGuzman's next book is released at www.chaneldeguzman.com.

You can also connect with Dr. DeGuzman here:

» *Blog: www.chaneldeguzman.com*
» *Twitter: twitter.com/chaneldeguzman*
» *Facebook: facebook.com/chaneldeguzman*